More Advance Praise ior
Be a Network Marketing Superstar:

"*Be a Network Marketing Superstar* is an absolute must for every direct seller's learning library. It's rich with time-tested strategies that will build a strong foundation for success and sprinkled with fresh ideas to give you that edge you need to move to the top of your pay plan. If you're ready to move to 'superstar' status with your company, get Mary's book right away!"
>   —Jane Deuber, Co-founder,
>   Direct Selling Women's Alliance

"*Be a Network Marketing Superstar* provides an excellent introduction to and overview of the direct selling industry as well as a clear method for succeeding in direct sales. Mary Christensen has created an excellent handbook that can be used for any direct selling business and any product. From attitude to actions, she outlines the steps to success. I believe that anyone who follows her formula will experience amazing results!"
>   —Rosemary Redmond, President, Weekenders USA

"*Be a Network Marketing Superstar* gives a step-by-step approach providing simple concepts that will guide a new or seasoned individual toward superstardom. The worksheets that follow each step are thought-provoking and excellent action steps."
>   —Dyan Lucero, President, Jafra Cosmetics

Be a Network Marketing
SUPERSTAR

The One Book You Need to Make More Money
Than You Ever Thought Possible

Mary Christensen
with
Wayne Christensen

American Management Association

New York • Atlanta • Brussels • Chicago • Mexico City • San Francisco
Shanghai • Tokyo • Toronto • Washington, D.C.

This publication is designed to provide accurate and authoritative information in regard to the subject matter covered. It is sold with the understanding that the publisher is not engaged in rendering legal, accounting, or other professional service. If legal advice or other expert assistance is required, the services of a competent professional person should be sought.

Library of Congress Cataloging-in-Publication Data

Christensen, Mary, 1951–
     Be a network marketing superstar : the one book you need to make more money than you ever thought possible / Mary Christensen with Wayne Christensen.
       p.   cm.
    Includes index.
    ISBN-10: 0-8144-7431-4 (pbk.)
    ISBN-13: 978-0-8144-7431-0 (pbk.)
    1. Multilevel marketing.   2. Direct marketing.   I. Christensen, Wayne, 1945–
II. Title.

    HF5415.126.C4878   2007
    658.8'72—dc22

                               2007000387

Printing number

10   9   8   7   6   5   4   3

For Samantha, Brayden, and Paige

CONTENTS

Foreword by Dianne Baldridge		ix
Acknowledgments		xiii
Introduction		1
Step One	Dare to Dream	6
Step Two	Set Your Sights	10
Step Three	Believe You Can	16
Step Four	Work the Plan	24
Step Five	Don't Reinvent the Wheel	37
Step Six	Take Charge	43
Step Seven	Work the Hours	46
Step Eight	Master Six Core Skills	52
Step Nine	Honor Your Planner	55
Step Ten	Sell, Don't Tell	60

Step Eleven	Radiate Positive Energy	66
Step Twelve	Focus on Relationships	70
Step Thirteen	Keep It Simple	75
Step Fourteen	Become an Effective Communicator	79
Step Fifteen	Keep Finding New People	83
Step Sixteen	Become a Mentor	89
Step Seventeen	Embrace the Tools	93
Step Eighteen	Keep Moving, Whatever Happens	97
Step Nineteen	Bend, Don't Break	101
Step Twenty	Manage Your Priorities	104
Step Twenty-One	Don't Let Fear Trample Your Dreams	109
Step Twenty-Two	Fix What's Faulty	114
Step Twenty-Three	Lead by Example	117
Step Twenty-Four	Keep Your Eye on the Ball	123
Step Twenty-Five	Never Stop Learning	127
Step Twenty-Six	Have Fun	130
A Few Final Thoughts		133
Index		135
About the Author		143

FOREWORD

I LOVE DIRECT SELLING! I guess you could say it's in my blood. I've been involved in one aspect of it or another for more than 30 years. And I've enjoyed every minute!

It's not how I started out or how I envisioned my life. I was a school librarian. When I attended my first direct selling "party," the consultant asked me if I wanted to be a consultant too. I told her no. I told her no several times. But one holiday season I decided to earn a little extra money, and the rest, as they say, is history—I was the top seller in the nation two years after I started; I set the all-time organizational development record for the nation; I was the president of a large direct selling company; and this year I founded my own direct selling company (Butterfly World-wide).

I'm so proud to have had a career in this amazing industry. (And by the way, my income through my years in direct selling was a "little" higher than what I would ever have earned as a librarian.) I'm sharing all this with you because it shows what direct sales can do for you and why I believe so strongly in the incredible opportunity this industry offers.

I was successful, yes, but wow do I wish I had had a book like *Be a Network Marketing Superstar* when I first started out in this business! If you are considering a career in direct selling, or if you are a direct seller already, this book can do wonders for you. Mary Christensen has taken her wealth of experience in our industry and boiled it down to an easy-to-read, easy-to-understand, yet profoundly complete guide to success.

Mary shows you how simple this business can be. I know thousands of people who are super successful in direct selling. They all started where you are right now: dreaming of making it big. Mary made it, and you can, too. She has laid out all the steps to success for you. She tells you where to concentrate your time and effort, how to build a team, how to be a great leader. She shares tips for mentoring your team to success and what to do to keep your business and your income growing. There's really nothing you need to be a successful direct selling entrepreneur that you won't find in the pages of *Be a Network Marketing Superstar*.

But this marvelous book is more than just a self-help handbook. It's also a workbook that will prepare you for the journey that lies ahead. At the end of each chapter you'll find questions that take what you just learned and help you apply it to the real world, *your* real world. They take all the great information from each chapter and help you apply it to, as Mary calls it, your own "Planet Reality." They're a wonderful first step to helping you build in the accountability you need to have—for yourself and to yourself—to be successful in this business.

I first met Mary Christensen when she was speaking at a Direct Selling Association Annual Meeting. Her talk was dynamic and inspiring and filled with great insights and training. She grabbed my attention from the moment she began talking and held my interest until she left the stage to the kind of animated applause you don't often hear at meetings like that. I hope you enjoy learning from Mary Christensen as she shares with you how to become a network marketing superstar. And I trust that, armed with the information you'll garner from this book, your direct selling career will be a huge success.

Dianne Baldridge
Founder and President, Butterfly Worldwide

ACKNOWLEDGMENTS

Thanks to our support team: Dane, Nikki, David, Beki, Tiffany, and Matt; Johanna and Stan Corbett; Dan Jensen of Jenetek; our agent, Ed Knappman of New England Publishing Associates; our editor, Ellen Kadin; and our publisher, AMACOM.

Be a Network Marketing
SUPERSTAR

INTRODUCTION

THERE IS NO "RESERVED" SIGN ON WEALTH. Anyone who wants it and is prepared to work for it can have it. Nor is there any rule that demands you choose between financial freedom and family life.

When I first stumbled onto network marketing (also known as direct selling, multilevel marketing, and MLM), I was looking for a way to support my two young children and a mortgage. I had no notion that it would change my life.

But it did. I found a way to become financially independent.

But that's not all. I discovered that I could have it both ways—the money and my life. Wealth, measured not only in dollar terms, but also in quality of life. Dreams truly can come true.

Anyone can dream. And anyone can realize those dreams, whatever his or her current skills, experiences, and circumstances. *Be a Network Marketing Superstar* will show you how, even on Planet Reality, where life doesn't always go the way we expect it to.

There are countless reasons why every week more than 175,000 people start a network marketing business in America, and 475,000 sign on worldwide. (The Direct Selling Association reports that there are over 14 million people involved in network marketing in America, and more than 54 million worldwide.)

In an increasingly uncertain world, more of us are seeking an alternative to the traditional pattern of study, work, and retire. Those willing to sacrifice family, friends, and leisure pursuits to the demands of a corporate employer are decreasing in number. Men and women alike are realizing that the best security in life is self-reliance. This shift in attitudes is having a profound effect, with a staggering increase in the number of people in the United States working from home compared to just five years ago.

Women's attitudes are changing just as fast. Although being a loving, involved parent is still the top priority for many women, fewer are prepared to gamble with their future and are making financial independence sit high on their list of priorities.

Although the dream of owning your own business is appealing, statistics paint a more realistic picture of long hours, high stress, and low returns for small- to medium-size business owners, who struggle to make a profit after deducting costs for leasing, inventory, staff, and operations.

The answer is network marketing, an opportunity to own your own business without taking on the burden of going it alone. It's an entrepreneur's dream.

Here's how network marketing works: As an independent representative (also known as a distributor, associate, consultant, member, or business owner) you form a partnership with a corporation that provides a product or service along with administrative and marketing support. With the corporation taking care of the back end of the business, you are free to focus on the frontline actions that produce income.

Your income comes from selling products or services, and from recruiting others to sell products or services. The higher your total sales, the higher your income.

What makes network marketing so attractive is that it costs almost nothing to start and very little to run. There is no up-front capital investment required, apart from a small outlay for a starter kit, so you can own your own business without using your own funds or having to borrow capital.

There is no ceiling on what you can earn, and you don't have to sacrifice family and friends to join the highest echelon of achievers.

Most network marketers run their business from home, and they work it around their everyday life. Some opt to supplement the household income by working their business part-time while they, their spouse, or both of them continue in traditional employment. For others, their network marketing business is the sole source of household income.

Couples pooling their skills and resources to build a network marketing business together are becoming more common, allowing family to take center stage in their lives.

No one way works better than others. The point of network marketing is to provide freedom and flexibility to fit your personal ambitions and circumstances. What counts is that you get to decide what's best for your life.

Network marketing is one of the few businesses where you can earn as you learn, right from the start. If you find yourself faltering:

★ Think of the millions who labor through years of university or college for a chance to join the ranks of the higher-income earners.

★ Think of the millions who invest their own capital in a business only to end up working horrendous hours trying to make it pay against all odds.

★ Think of those who waste their life stuck in traffic, as they commute to the office and back.

✶ Think of those who miss pivotal events in their children's lives, due to work commitments.

✶ Think of those who dread going to work each day to boring, repetitive jobs, not to mention having to work with and for people they wouldn't spend time with under any other circumstances.

✶ Think how lucky you are that you are at the helm of your own low-risk, high-reward business—business where you get to decide how your time will be spent and with whom you will spend it.

I have written *Be a Network Marketing Superstar* for everyone who is serious about making his or her dream for a network marketing business a financial and lifestyle reality. If you are prepared to move out of your comfort zone and commit to making it work, whatever your current situation, I will show you how to join the hundreds of thousands of people who enjoy a fabulous income and a dream lifestyle from their network marketing business: Wealth in the true spirit of the word.

Here are the three basic principles of network marketing:

1. *There are no shortcuts.* As with any endeavor, if you want to succeed you must be prepared to work hard, and work smart. And that starts with mastering the skills that have been proven to work by the millions who have already built successful businesses.

2. *There are no excuses.* If something isn't working for you, you have to be prepared to change. That doesn't mean looking around for a better company, a better system, or a new idea. It means changing *you.* Perhaps your attitude, the way you present yourself, the way you communicate, or your understanding of how the business works. This book will help you determine where to focus your time, energy, and resources to enhance your chance of success.

3. *There are no trophies for trying.* Network marketing re-

wards results. Not everyone will make it because not everyone is prepared to do what it takes. If you *are* prepared, the rewards you receive will make it all worthwhile. If you decide network marketing is not for you, you will have risked nothing and lost nothing. One of the strengths of the industry is that you can even keep your regular job while you are building your business.

This book will complement your corporate partner's training program, which will give you specific information and guidance related to your products and your business opportunity. Rather than replicate information you will find in company manuals and learn at company-run seminars, I will focus on how to apply what you read in your manuals and hear at training programs. Believe me, there is a wide gap between the theory of network marketing and what you will discover when you get out into the real world, or Planet Reality.

Follow it as a handbook and it will guide you step by step toward your most ambitious goals. A worksheet follows each chapter to help you apply what you read. Although knowledge is a powerful asset, knowledge translated into action is the winning formula.

Above all, believe you can do it. I know you can because I know how few skills and what little confidence I had when I started. Every step you are about to take, I have taken, as have the millions who are now enjoying the rewards they worked hard for. Rewards that are waiting for you.

Welcome to a dynamic industry. If you are willing to learn and willing to work, you will create the life you and your family deserve and become a role model for others who dare to dream big dreams.

Dare to Dream

IMAGINE YOU HAVE BEEN GRANTED THREE WISHES.
What will you wish for?

> More excitement? More adventure? More freedom?
> More money? More time?
> More fun?

The only limit to what we can achieve in life is the limit of our imagination. Every achiever—from the scientist who achieves a medical breakthrough that saves millions of lives, to the sportsman who overcomes all odds to break a world record—started with a dream.

Imagine the first settlers to land on American soil knowing next to nothing about what they would find here, but with hearts bursting with dreams for a better future.

Imagine the first person to gaze up into the night sky and dream of landing on the moon. At the time, it must have seemed beyond impossible. But it happened, because someone dared to dream.

Life is not about following a path that others set for us. It's about blazing new trails to create the life we choose.

Dreaming frees us from our doubts, our skepticism, our prejudices, our past experiences, and the expectations of others, to reveal the truth of what we want in life. Our capacity to achieve has no limit, if we dare to dream big dreams.

Take time to consider what will make you, and those you love, truly happy. Ask six simple questions:

1. What do I want to be?
2. What do I want to do?
3. What do I want to give?
4. What do I want to have?
5. How do I want to spend my time?
6. With whom do I want to spend my time?

When you know the answer to these questions, you gain awesome power over your future.

However long it takes for you to decide how you want to live your life, it will be time well spent, because when you know what matters most to you, you will move mountains to make it happen. Lackluster dreams never inspired great deeds or amazing feats.

Think how we respond to events that touch our hearts. Think how we rally behind our favorite causes. Think of the lengths you would go to protect your family and the people you love. The more passion you have, the more energy you will generate to make your dreams come true.

Too many people live in a drab world of black and white. Too many allow self-doubt and uncertainty to quash their dreams. Not you. Think vivid, vibrant color.

If you dream of sending your kids to the best schools, imagine them walking through the gates and attending classes. Imagine your pride when they graduate among their peers.

If you dream about a new car, imagine the color of the paint, the sound of the engine, the smell of new leather seats. Visualize the trips you will take and the adventures you will enjoy.

If you dream of helping others, picture the difference you will make in their lives.

If your dream is a new home, walk your imagination through every room. Let your bare feet glide on the wooden floors and sink into the soft carpet. Picture the shade of the walls. Feel the texture of the furnishings. Gaze at the view from the windows.

If you dream of traveling the world, think of the sights, sounds, and tastes that you will savor along the way.

This is not the time to hold back. Set your imagination free and let it soar.

✯   ✯   ✯   ✯   ✯   ✯

If you have chosen network marketing as your vehicle for realizing your dreams, you have chosen well. You will have an incredible journey as you navigate toward the future you dream of. You will almost certainly encounter roadblocks as you progress toward where you want, and deserve, to be. This, after all, is Planet Reality. Knowing *why* you are doing what you are doing is more important than knowing *how* when you are tested. When you know what you are working for, whatever happens along the way, your passion will propel you forward.

Some people see things as they are and say, "Why?"
I dream things that never were and say, "Why not?"

—GEORGE BERNARD SHAW

. . . .
WORKSHEET ONE: DARE TO DREAM
. . . .

Conjure up your personal genie and grant yourself three wishes. Bring them alive with as much detail as you can imagine.

My first dream is

_____

_____

_____

My second dream is

_____

_____

_____

My third dream is

_____

_____

_____

Set Your Sights

NOW IT'S TIME TO TURN YOUR DREAMS INTO GOALS.
Dreaming kindles our imagination and ignites our passion,
but goals are tangible destinations that we set before we set
out on our journey. Knowing what you are working toward
will focus your energies in the right direction and keep you
on the right track.

The purpose of a goal is to take you from where you are
to where you want to be. Therefore goals have to be realistic.
That doesn't mean forgetting your dreams, but rather setting
progressive goals, or mileposts, that will take you toward
them, one step at a time. I recommend that you set your
first goals no more than one year ahead. There will be time
to focus on new goals once you achieve these first ones.

No matter how impatient you are to start work, know
that one of the most common mistakes made by entrepreneurs and corporate businesspeople alike is being impatient.

The time you spend identifying your priorities is never wasted. Having the discipline to clarify your goals is one of the keys to success.

Take these seven actions to set your goals for the next twelve months:

1. Define each goal as a measurable destination, with a specific deadline. For example: "By June 30 next year I will be earning $5,000 per month," or "By June 30 next year I will have $20,000 saved toward my first investment property."

2. Rate each goal on a priority scale of 1 (low) to 5 (high) by asking yourself, "How important is this goal to my ultimate dream?" Make sure these are your goals, not goals set to please or impress someone else. This is your life, and you won't be happy living someone else's dream.

3. Choose only the goals that you rated the highest. Reconsider any goal that you have rated below 3, asking, "Is this what I truly want?"

4. Make sure you have not included an escape route ("I'll give it my best for six months . . ."), you have not involved others who do not share your passion ("If my partner will agree to baby-sit more, I will . . ."), and you can achieve each goal without conditions ("If my boss will agree to cut back my hours . . .").

5. A goal is a commitment. It only has value if you promise that within the time frame you have set you will have achieved it. Be specific. The less ambiguous, confusing, or open-ended your goal is, the better. Make sure you can answer two key questions about each goal:

    a. "What is going to change?"

    b. "When will the change be complete?"

6. Check that your goals are compatible. Ask yourself, "Can I achieve every one of my goals in the time I have?" If not, make a choice right now about what matters most. The more goals you set, the less likely you are to achieve any of them. For example, if you are a bit of a couch potato, and

one of your goals is to run a marathon while the other is to double your income in a year, you should be seeing a red flag, not a checkered one. Both goals will take single-minded dedication. It is better to choose one and soften the other. For example, make the business goal your top priority, and postpone the marathon, amending that goal to building your fitness until you are able to run five miles three times a week.

7. Consider your goals against your current circumstances. Check that you have not set yourself up to fail with overly ambitious goals if you are already highly committed. For instance, if you are busy raising a young family, you could start working toward your dream of a mortgage-free home by reducing your mortgage by 20 percent or paying off your credit cards.

Ask yourself, "Are my goals realistic in my current situation?" If you set your sights too high, you will quickly become disillusioned. Success is a great motivator. It's better to set modest goals and achieve them than to overextend yourself and fail. As your circumstances change, so can your goals. As you achieve each goal, set your next one until, step by step, you find yourself stepping into your dream.

. . . .
WORKSHEET **TWO** : SET YOUR SIGHTS
. . . .

1. Write out your goals, giving each goal a completion date. List as many as you like. When you have finished, review each goal and rate it according to how important it is to you (1 = highest priority; 5 = lowest priority).

I will:

_____

By: _____ *Rating:* _____

I will:

_____

By: _____ *Rating:* _____

I will:

_____

By: _____ *Rating:* _____

I will:

_____

By: _____ *Rating:* _____

I will:

_____

By: _____ *Rating:* _____

I will:

_____

By: _____ *Rating:* _____

2. Rearrange your goals in order of priority:

    1: _____

    2: _____

    3: _____

    4: _____

5: _____

6: _____

3. Put your goals through the reality checks outlined in actions 3 to 7 on pages 11 and 12.

4. Rewrite your two top goals:

My most important goal is:

_____

My deadline to complete this goal is:

_____

My second most important goal is:

_____

My deadline to complete this goal is:

_____

5. Bring your goals to life with pictures, such as a photo of the school your children will attend, the dream home you will build, the car you will buy, your ultimate vacation destination, or the child you will sponsor.

6. Print five copies of your top goals. Spread them around you—on your bathroom mirror, on the dash-board of your car, on the inside front cover of your plan-ner, next to your computer, near the phone, or on the door of your refrigerator; in other words, anyplace where you tend to spend much of your time.

7. Look at your goals every day, as many times as you can, always putting yourself in the picture. See yourself traveling to meet your child, sitting in the driver's seat of the car with your hands on the steering wheel; lying back on a recliner at a beach resort as you watch your children frolic in the pool; or feeling the pride well up as you watch your child graduate.

three

Believe You Can

HENRY FORD IS QUOTED AS SAYING, "If you think you can, or think you can't, you are right." He was right.

Belief is the fuel that drives network marketers and you will be as strong or as weak as you believe yourself to be. You need:

* ⋆ Belief in your business
* ⋆ Belief in the company you choose to partner with
* ⋆ Belief in the products you represent
* ⋆ But most of all . . . belief in yourself!

When you believe in yourself, you free yourself from the expectations and actions of others and equip yourself to deal with the inevitable swings and roundabouts of normal business growth.

Self-doubt will slow you down. If you unload your

doubts before you get started you will be able to move faster and more smoothly toward your goals.

It's easy to say, "Believe in yourself," but many of us harbor feelings of doubt or inadequacy. So let's look at how you acquired your beliefs in the first place.

Beliefs were most likely formed when you were young—from messages sent to you by your parents and other influential people in your life, such as your peers and teachers.

Not all of us had the good fortune to grow up in a nurturing environment surrounded by people who knew the importance of building self-esteem. People who cared about us may have sent the wrong messages from inexperience, or because they were mirroring their own insecurities.

Others of us, despite having the advantage of loving support, may have been selective in what we chose to hear or remember. For a variety of reasons, perhaps because we weren't one of the cool kids in school, we began attaching negative labels to ourselves. Before we knew it, these labels stuck fast.

Whatever your past experiences, you can start cleaning your slate whenever you want. It may take time, but every step is ground that you have gained from your enemy—lack of belief in yourself and in your right to have, and be, the best.

You can start by accepting that belief comes from within, and taking responsibility for your feelings of strength or inadequacy. As an adult you are free to form your own beliefs. Your past is in the past. You are now in control of your life.

Ninety percent of all communication is self-talk. Playing negative tapes over and over inside your mind will only deepen the groove of negativity in your brain and stifle your ability to achieve your goals. You may as well play positive ones (would you force yourself to listen to bad music or to a talk-back host whose opinions made you angry?)

Start by listing all your great qualities—your warmth, your compassion, your vision, your honesty, your intelligence, or your creativity. Look for areas where you excel. Think of what a loving parent, partner, son or daughter, or friend you are. Think of the determination, focus, and energy that have brought you to this point in your life and all the good things you have done. Think of where you started and how far you have already traveled in life.

Filter criticism. If it's valid, thank the person who did you a favor (even if it doesn't feel like it at the time) and consider it a chance to grow. For example, let's say you've been told you are too lazy to build a successful network marketing business. But wait. The problem may not be laziness. Lazy people don't start their own businesses or set goals to change their lives. It may simply be that you are overwhelmed with responsibilities or carrying unresolved issues that sap your energy. In that case, take a step back, and decide what's important in your life, and what you need to let go.

You are not your blunders or slipups. The only people who get things right all the time are those who play it safe and never attempt anything new. Can you imagine anything worse? You deserve a more exciting, fulfilling life than that, even if that does mean risking a few spills.

Remind yourself that the judgment of others will be clouded by their own personalities and experiences. You are you: unique and wonderful! You can be whatever you want to be, have whatever you want to have, and live the life that you thought only dreams were made of when you believe in yourself.

If you are among people who make you feel insecure, start to loosen ties with them and seek out positive, enthusiastic, and supportive people instead.

Top up your self-esteem with every positive feedback and compliment you receive. By filtering out the bad and absorbing the good, you will become stronger emotionally. Forgive those who hurt you, whether or not they meant to, and move on.

We like people who like us, so be considerate of the feelings of others and interested in their lives. Be generous with
compliments. You know how harmful thoughtlessness, indif-
ference, and gossip can be. You have to have a clear con-
science before you can achieve true self-esteem.

Above all, learn to separate fact from fantasy. We have
two sides to our brain: rational and emotional. Our *emotional*
side is reactive and helps us respond swiftly to potential dan-
ger. When there is no real threat we sometimes allow our
emotional side to create unnecessary stress.

Our *rational* side is proactive. We use it to make decisions
and solve problems based on reason rather than emotion.
We are using the rational side of our brain when we question
the beliefs we hold about ourselves. Learn to differentiate
between the two when you find yourself under pressure. Try
to put a distance between the issue and the resolution. Time
is a great clarifier.

Make a conscious decision to be as kind to yourself as
you are to others. Don't waste time wallowing in past mistakes, and focus instead on the person you will become. Just
because you couldn't do something before, doesn't mean you
can't do it now. Tell yourself, "That was then, this is now."
You can't drive forward if your eyes are fixed on the rearview
mirror.

If you have genuine personal issues to deal with, don't
despair.

You most likely have heard that Michelangelo created his
perfect statue of *David* from just one block of marble. But
you may not know he didn't start with perfect marble. Two
artists had already discarded the block because of imperfec-
tions they believed would prevent them from achieving a
quality sculpture. I guess Michelangelo knew what we should
also know: It's not what you start with; it's what you make
of what you have that makes the difference.

Nobody is perfect. Focus on your strengths, and allow
yourself to grow as you build your business and your life.

Identify weaknesses and start working on them. Negative thinking without a specific plan for improvement is self-destructive and pointless. That's why we call it *stinking thinking!*

The good news is that I have met very few network marketers who have not experienced incredible personal growth as they worked toward their goals. What matters is that you are willing to move forward. It takes courage to change your life. Confidence will come when you start to see results. Courage first, then confidence.

You will need to be strong, because it is the nature of network marketing that we continually have to put ourselves on the line. Rejection goes with the territory. You can't avoid rebuffs or mistakes, but by believing in yourself you will be able to weather good times and bad.

Building a healthy self-esteem is not just about you. Your confidence will filter down through your organization as it grows. By working on your self-belief you are not only helping yourself, you are developing skills that will enable you to help others. The more strength you have within, the more you will have to give and the more likely you are to build an organization of loyal, committed people.

WORKSHEET **THREE**: BELIEVE YOU CAN

1. Make a list of your positive qualities. Be generous in your praise, as you would be if people you care about asked you to say what you most admired about them. Don't stop until you have listed at least ten qualities. If you need help (no false modesty allowed), ask family and friends what they like, respect, and admire about you.

1: _____

2: _____

3: _____

4: _____

5: _____

6: _____

7: _____

8: _____

9: _____

10: _____

2. Consider how each of these qualities will help you achieve your goals, and write them as statements of fact. For example, "My determination to succeed will ensure I make twenty calls a day regardless of other commitments I have."

1: _____

2: _____

3: _____

4: _____

5: _____

6: _____

7: _____

8: _____

9: _____

10: _____

3. List any lingering self-doubts that may limit your progress (you can skip this step if you are one of the lucky few with an abundance of self-confidence). If you need

more than a few lines, you are probably indulging your-self in a little pity party. Reread the chapter before you reach for another page.

1: _____

2: _____

3: _____

4: _____

4. Challenge each of your doubts, using rational rather than emotional responses. Ask:

"Is this belief valid, or is it stinking thinking?"

"Does it stand up to scrutiny, or am I using it as a convenient excuse?"

"Is this about my personality, or about a behavior I can change?"

5. If you still have some issues on your mind, it's time to test whether you are passionate about your goals or just playing with them. Answer this question truthfully (if you don't, you're only kidding yourself):

"Am I prepared to sacrifice my dreams for perceptions or mistakes that belong in the past or am I willing to let go and move on?"

6. Are you ready to move on and start on your goals? Make a commitment to address behaviors that will hold you back. For example:

I will become more organized by

_____

I will overcome my shyness by

_____

I will forgive

_____

I will stop

_____

I will start

_____

I will become

_____

7. Reread all the nice things you said about yourself and remember all the nice things other people have said about you. Do this over and over, especially whenever you feel a ping of self-doubt. Your confidence will strengthen as you start getting results.

Work the Plan

WHEN YOU ARE CLEAR ABOUT WHAT YOU ARE WORK-ING FOR, you are ready to focus on how you are going to get it. It's time to take a look at how different companies pay their representatives.

Every network marketing company has a compensation plan (sometimes called a marketing plan) that sets out clearly what you have to do to get what you want.

The common denominator of all legitimate plans (i.e., plans other than illegitimate "pyramid schemes," which are discussed at the end of Step Four) is that payments are based on the sales you generate, both from personal sales and the sales of people you recruit. The higher your total sales, the more you will earn. If you are lucky, the plan will be simple and easy to understand. But many plans seem confusing and complicated, especially to newcomers. Compounding the

problem is that many are bogged down by insider-speak, or
jargon.

Don't be deterred. As the business has developed, so have
the plans. Most good ones specifically focus on key behaviors
required to build a successful downline organization. A
strong *downline*—that is, the people you recruit and train
and from whose sales you also earn a commission—is at the
heart of success. As you learn the plan, you are learning what
you must do to maximize your income.

If you understand the plan you can explain it clearly and
enthusiastically to prospective recruits. When you do a good
job they, in turn, will be able to explain it clearly and enthusiastically to their prospective recruits. Now your entire organization is focusing on the most productive areas.

This is what you need to know regardless of what plan
you are working with:

The most basic principle of network marketing is duplication—selling product, and recruiting others to sell product
and recruit others, over and over and over. This is what all
plans are designed to encourage and reward.

You will be paid a percentage of the total sales you generate, usually monthly, although some companies work on
four-week, two-week, or one-week cycles.

Your percentage will increase as you reach and maintain
higher levels (also known as ranks). This is designed to encourage you to build your business and reward you for consistent performance.

Your rank is based on your personal sales and the sales
of everyone you recruit, both directly (known as first levels)
and indirectly (the people your first levels recruit down the
line, known as second and third levels, etc). Collectively,
these people are known as your personal group (or downline).

When a member of your group recruits enough people
and produces enough sales to achieve a higher rank, they are

known as a *breakaway*. You are paid on your breakaways, but at a lower rate, as the leader of that group is expected to support her or his own people, freeing you to find and develop more recruits.

Most plans require that you maintain a higher rank than your breakaways. This makes sense, as otherwise one person could rise through the ranks on the efforts of one successful recruit. The smartest way to maintain your higher rank and protect your income is to recruit and develop lots of first levels.

Those who develop the most breakaways reach the highest ranks of most plans—and consequently the highest rewards. A few superachievers receive *monthly* payments of hundreds of thousands of dollars or more. But they earned their rank the way you must, by recruiting one person at a time. How quickly you reach each rank will depend on how hard you work and how skilled you are at marketing your products and your business opportunity.

If you grow your business steadily, your income will rise month by month, subject to the fluctuating demand for your products throughout the year.

★ ★ ★ ★ ★ ★

Most companies allocate approximately the same percentage of total sales to pay their representatives. However, each company structures its plan slightly differently. As one example, some plans pay a small percentage on the sales of everyone you recruit, whereas others require that you recruit a set number of people and reach a combined sales target before you are paid on your recruits. Another example is the difference in how much you have to sell personally to earn higher commissions.

The four most common plans currently in use (making up 98 percent of all plans) are:

1. Stairstep or Breakaway
2. Hybrid Unilevel or Unigen

3. Forced Matrix
4. Binary

Don't be put off by the titles. They simply depict the structure of each plan. The following brief description of each will help you make sense of them:

Stairstep or Breakaway Plans

Stairstep or Breakaway Plans have been around the longest and are used by approximately 62 percent of companies. The key details are:

* There is no limit on how many people you can recruit.
* There is no limit on how many people you may have as first levels (your top line).
* Your personal recruits (first-level) form a new line (or leg).
* The people they recruit become your second levels, third levels, etc.
* You earn commission on your personal group (your top line and the people they recruit).
* To qualify for commission you are expected to meet a monthly personal and group target.
* You climb "stairs" to qualify at each level, where you are rewarded by higher percentages.
* You earn commission on your breakaway groups (legs that achieve a higher rank) as long as you stay ahead of them by being promoted to a higher rank yourself.
* The more first-level recruits you have, the stronger your business will be, because when one recruit breaks away you have others to maintain the balance.

Companies using Stairstep or Breakaway Plans include Amway and Mary Kay.

Hybrid Unilevel or Unigen Plans

Hybrid Unilevel or Unigen Plans are used by approximately 18 percent of companies. The key details are:

* ★ Similarly to Stairstep/Breakaway Plans, Hybrid Unilevel or Unigen Plans pay commission on personal and breakaway groups.
* ★ You are encouraged to recruit your customers, who are commonly known as Associates or Members.
* ★ Associates receive wholesale buying privileges and may order directly from the company. Although they mostly buy for themselves, some service a small customer base.
* ★ You generally earn a higher commission on personal recruits than with other types of plans.

Nu Skin is an example of a company using this type of plan.

Forced Matrix Plans

Forced Matrix Plans are used by about 12 percent of companies. The key details are:

* ★ There is a limit to how many people you may personally recruit across your top line (this is known as a limited matrix).
* ★ Your personal recruits are one line below you, meaning your direct recruits are known as your second lev-

els, your second level recruits are known as your third levels, etc.

* The number of downline levels (called depth) you may have is also capped.

* Any people you recruit over your limit will drop a level. This is known as *spillover*.

Melaleuca is one example of a company with a Forced Matrix Plan.

Binary Plans

Binary Plans are used by about 6 percent of companies. The key details are:

* You can only recruit two people, or legs, as your first levels.

* Any additional first-level recruits become your second levels, etc.

* You are paid on the sales of the weaker of your two legs.

* You may be allowed to carry unpaid sales forward.

* Some plans allow you to form a second matrix.

An example of a company with a Binary Plan is USANA.

★ ★ ★ ★ ★ ★

Confused? You won't be the first, or the last, to find compensation plans complicated. But don't give up.

Understanding Your Plan

Remember when you decided to take the test for your driver's license? No doubt you found the handbook full of numbing facts, figures, distances, speeds, and signals, but you wanted your license, so you studied it so you could pass the test. Once you started to drive, it all began to make sense and made life on the road much easier, because you knew what to do.

It's the same with the plan. You only have to learn it once, and it will fall into place as you put it into practice. Taking the time to understand your plan will give you the knowledge and confidence to share it with others. A cursory knowledge of other types of plans may help you deal with questions from prospective recruits.

To separate the key points of your plan from the quagmire of jargon and hype, look for the answers to these questions:

* What will I be paid on my personal sales?
* How much must I personally sell to earn the highest commission on my sales?
* What will I be paid on my first-level recruits, that is, the people I personally recruit?
* What will I be paid on my personal group, that is, including my indirect recruits (the people recruited by the people I personally recruit)?
* How much must my group sales total for me to earn the highest commission on its sales?
* What will I be paid on my breakaway groups?
* What do I have to do to be paid on my breakaway groups?
* What will I be paid on my total business?

Additional questions to ask yourself are:

* What level on the plan will I aim for?
* What do I have to do to reach that level?

The most appealing aspect of all plans is that they clearly mark out key mileposts en route to your destination. Once you calculate how much time you will allocate to your business and factor in your current skill level, you will be able to set a realistic rank to aim for in your first year. This will enable you to calculate your income.

Comparing Other Plans

If you are comparing plans from different companies, make sure you compare apples with apples. Here are a couple of examples:

Some plans pay out on wholesale figures (the price you pay for product), while others pay out on retail (the price your customer pays). If your wholesale price is 80 percent of retail, then being paid 25 percent on the wholesale price is the same as being paid 20 percent on the retail price of your products.

Some plans quote discount, while others quote markup. Being paid on 30 percent discount is the same as being paid on 43 percent markup.

To add further confusion, some companies work their plan on a points system rather than prices. This helps to equalize the payout across different countries, economies, exchange rates, and prices. These companies tend to allow or encourage you to build your business in a number of countries.

Although this sounds great if you have friends and family in other countries, it is easier said than done. One reason is that the prospect of an international business may distract you from your business at home. I have seen many businesses fail because the leaders spread themselves too thin. Another is the expense of traveling to other countries. The upshot is that successful international businesses are usually built by people who already have mature businesses in one country or who have strong ties to both.

Be wary of companies that claim their plan pays more than others. It is not uncommon (although it is unethical) for overeager representatives to trumpet their plan as superior to another, but if you take a closer look you may discover that both produce the same end results. A few use confusing terminology that disguises actual percentages paid. Most plans include subtle "breaks" to control the total payout, which may not be evident to the uninitiated.

Find out what percentage of sales comes from representatives selling to their customers. If most sales are made that way, then you have a greater chance of earning income from selling the product. If most of the sales are made solely to representatives who use the product personally, like a buying club, then you may have trouble selling enough to make a reasonable income.

Look for a plan that offers a good chance of earning at least $25 and, ideally, $35 an hour, from the start. Any lesser amount will make it hard for you and the people you recruit to stick with it. Representatives who make money at the outset stay longer, and your chances of building a viable business increase.

Most companies offer between 20 percent and 50 percent discount off retail to representatives. A 25 percent discount means that you can purchase $100 retail price for $75 wholesale. This is where most new representatives make their income. It can take months of consistent recruiting for their commission check to grow enough to produce a reasonable monthly income.

Be wary also of companies that encourage representatives to buy large amounts of product at the outset. This is called front-end loading. Most people will have trouble selling the product to others and it ends up gathering dust in their basement or garage.

Make sure you check out the refund policy before you sign. Both the DSA Code of Ethics and many state laws require companies to offer no less than a 90 percent refund for returned product in resalable condition if it has been purchased within the last twelve months. Scam companies don't offer this or don't follow through even if they do offer it.

Don't be deterred. You wouldn't start a new job without making sure you know what you will be paid. Your plan is the blueprint for your business. Understanding it is integral to your success.

I recommend you choose a reputable company (checking to see whether it is a member of the Direct Selling Association is a good place to start) and make your decision based on your passion for the products and mission. If those elements are right, the plan will fall into place for you.

If you can't get your heart into the products and mission, then no plan will be enough to keep you enthused. Money is important, but it is seldom the only reason people are in the business.

Pyramid Schemes

Despite the vigilance of federal and state prosecutors, there are a small number of operations posing as legitimate network marketing companies that are actually illegal pyramid schemes. This is what you should know about these schemes.

Any plan that primarily rewards people for recruiting, rather than selling goods and services, is a pyramid scheme. Although pyramid schemes are illegal in most countries worldwide, they still pop up from time to time.

Some are presented as "games" to trap the unwary, such as the airplane game, which encouraged participants to sell imaginary seats in an imaginary airplane. Once your airplane was full, you collected the money, while all those who bought seats tried to fill their own plane. It sounds nonsensical, as there was no value whatsoever in terms of products or services, but it worked because people succumbed to greed.

Gold coins sold as collector items and priced above their actual value was another scheme that trapped many people, making the originators rich, while all the other participants lost their money.

Why do people allow themselves to be taken in by such schemes? Because they offer very high commissions and bonuses often based on how much product is bought at the entry level.

Most countries clamp down heavily on these fraudulent "get-rich-quick'" schemes, by which the unscrupulous take advantage of the greedy, the lazy, and the naïve. Consumer protection agencies, and the Direct Selling Association, watch out for and report these schemes to state and federal prosecutors. And here's a warning: Not only the perpetrators, but also the participants, can be and are being prosecuted for their involvement in pyramid schemes.

The bottom line: If the deal seems to good to be true it probably is. Don't put your credibility and reputation on the line by falling for a "get-rich-quick" scheme that will most likely lose money for you and the people who trusted you.

. . . .
WORKSHEET **FOUR**: WORK THE PLAN
. . . .

1. Ask the person who recruited you to explain the compensation plan as simply as possible. You may find diagrams easier than words, words, and more words (imagine the nightmare your driver's manual would be for you without a few strategically placed diagrams).

2. Keep asking questions until you are satisfied you understand the basic concept of the plan. You do not need an encyclopedic knowledge but you do need a working

knowledge of the document that tells you how you will be paid.

3. If the person who recruited you is struggling to explain the plan to your satisfaction and cannot produce someone who can, call your corporate office support line for help.

4. Read the plan over and over until you "get it," especially up to the first two to three levels. As you read through it, make a list of questions to follow up with your corporate office or your upline (your *upline* is the person who recruited you).

5. Practice presenting the plan to friends and family members. Do it well and you may find yourself a new recruit or two from your practice group!

6. Plot your first twelve months by making these decisions:
   a. What monthly income will I be earning in twelve months?
   b. What rank must I reach to achieve this income?
   c. What must I do to reach this rank?
   d. How much time must I invest to reach and maintain this rank, factoring in a buffer zone for "Murphy's Law" delays?

7. Set yourself a weekly personal sales target and a monthly personal recruiting target based on where you want to be and how quickly you want to get there. Until

you have stepped up to the next level you can only guess-timate your group sales. Not all recruits will duplicate your results. Much will depend on how good you are at finding quality recruits. That's why it's best to focus on personal activity.

five

Don't Reinvent the Wheel

**WHEN YOU SIGNED THE INDEPENDENT REPRESENTA-
TIVE AGREEMENT** to start your own business, you probably
heard, "You are in business for yourself, but not by yourself."
That pretty much sums up what network marketing is
about.

Although you are 100 percent responsible for your results, you selected a corporation to be your business partner.
Whatever your reason—you fell in love with the product,
you liked the plan, or someone offered you a great opportunity—you are now in a powerful partnership.

Unlike the majority of self-employed who struggle to
build their business with borrowed capital and high over-
heads, you now have a partner with enormous resources all
at your disposal. You are effectively running a small business
with all the resources of a large one. Maximize your advantage by making the most of all that is available to you. You
pay only for the resources you need, so there is no waste.

Your future and that of your corporate partner are linked. The more successful you are, the more successful the corporation will be. The corporation wants you to succeed.

It's important that both sides establish and maintain a good relationship based on mutual understanding, trust, respect, and loyalty.

Each corporation is unique, with its own culture, products, plan, track record, and role models—all of which are living proof that the system works. From day one, you have access to this reservoir of resources. Seize that advantage.

You may not like everything your corporate partner does. Remember that the corporation is in partnership with a wide range of representatives, each with different goals and circumstances. It is unrealistic to expect everything to fit your specific needs.

As with any business, mistakes may be made from time to time. These are not deliberate (chances are you will make a few too). Have faith in your choice of company. Slipups are frustrating but they are not the end of the world unless you choose to make them so.

For example, a popular product that suddenly goes on back order is an inconvenience, but it is also an opportunity to trumpet the soaring demand for the product to your customers and recommend they keep an extra one handy, or order sooner during promotions (when popular products are promoted, sales often exceed company forecasts).

Cultivate a good relationship with the person who recruited you (your upline) and the people farther up the line who recruited that person. They all have a wealth of knowledge and experience to share with you through training and mentoring. They want you to succeed—the more successful you are, the more successful they will be. By learning to accept differences and avoid judgments you will foster great relationships with a myriad of personalities.

Above all, don't try to reinvent the wheel. Adopt your corporate partner's system. It has worked for others before you. Learn it, follow it, and duplicate it by example and through training.

Don't waste time creating your own resources. You have talented staff to do that for you in your corporate office—free!

The more time you spend at the frontline of your business, marketing your products and your business opportunity person-to-person, face-to-face, by phone, and by e-mail, the faster you will rise through the ranks. Time spent on activities that do not lead to recruiting, booking appointments, or selling product is time wasted.

★ ★ ★ ★ ★ ★

However ambitious your goals are, your business will be built one person at a time, through both direct and indirect recruits. As I have already explained, the key to success is duplication. If you decide to do things differently from the norm, you will complicate the business and confuse the people you recruit. Imagine what could happen if everybody you recruited created a different system. Confusion does not lead to sustained success. Look at McDonald's as an example. One system duplicated 17,000 times in America and 26,000 times all over the world. Or look at Starbucks. Or Curves.

Your job is to drive the system, not invent it.

Think of your business as a train. You are driving your train toward an incredible destination. Your corporate partner has laid the tracks, and others have traveled them before you. But you are the driver of this train and you're fired up with belief in yourself, your products, and your business opportunity.

The stations along the way are your mileposts, where you will celebrate your progress before setting out on the next leg of your journey. You started your network marketing business to build a fabulous income *and* a fabulous life. Celebrating the journey is part of the joy of success.

This is not a journey to take alone. The more people

who travel with you, the more quickly you will reach your destination. When you first set out, your train is hauling empty cars, ready to be filled with new recruits. As you bring more recruits on board, and as their belief and excitement add fuel to fire your engine, the more exhilarating your journey will be.

Invite as many people as you can. Don't prejudge and don't slow down for procrastinators. The longer you stop, the longer your journey will be, and the more frustrating it will be for those who have already joined. No one enjoys waiting and no one likes delays.

Don't worry about reaching capacity. The more people you recruit, the more it is likely that leaders will emerge to take charge of their own car. These breakaways will stay coupled to your engine as long as you keep filling more cars.

Some people will be with you for the long haul, while others will travel only a short distance. Don't fret when they leave early on. Network marketing is not a fail-safe system. It's an opportunity, and the reality is that half the people who start a business give up within the first three months.

Accept that everyone you recruit will have different ambitions, abilities, and circumstances. However far they travel with you, every one of them will enhance your journey.

Bon voyage!

WORKSHEET **FIVE**: DON'T REINVENT THE WHEEL

1. What is special about your company? Base your answer on your personal experiences, not on company literature.

_____

_____

_____

2. Who would be most interested in your business opportunity?

_____

_____

_____

3. Why?

_____

_____

_____

4. How will you reach these hot prospects?

_____

_____

_____

_____

5. What does your prospect get when he or she signs the agreement? Here's an example of what may be included in the starter kit:

- ★ A starter pack of our top selling products worth over $300
- ★ Two full-day training seminars
- ★ A 200-page business manual
- ★ Enough literature for your first month
- ★ A free gift valued at $50 when you place your first order within your first two weeks
- ★ A free gift worth $75 when you introduce a friend in your first thirty days

- ★ The chance to earn another $500 of products in our fast-start program
- ★ A monthly magazine
- ★ The support of an amazing team of people to help you
- ★ The chance to start immediately achieving a free trip to Hawaii
- ★ . . . all for a onetime investment of $250!

Write out your list here:

_____

_____

_____

_____

_____

_____

_____

_____

_____

_____

_____

6. What ongoing support can your new recruit expect?

_____

_____

_____

_____

Take Charge

HOWEVER GOOD YOUR COMPANY, your products, or your plan, your success is up to you—100 percent.

The only person who can guarantee you will achieve your goals is the person who owns them—you. From Day One, you are founder, president, and CEO of your own business.

There may be no "I" in team, but there is in win. Nor is there any limit to what you can achieve when you seize control.

By taking responsibility, you're not vulnerable to the performance of others, and you're free to focus on what you need to do to achieve your goals.

When things go well, this will be easy. But what about when things don't go according to plan? Do you have the strength and courage to accept responsibility through good times and bad?

Think of your train. Without a driver, it's going nowhere. Without a driver who knows where he's going, it may head up the wrong tracks. You can't drive your train from a seat in one of the cars. You have to sit up front with your hands firmly on the controls.

Life is not perfect, and it is unrealistic to believe that everything will go your way all the time. You will get your share of good luck, just as you will get your share of bad.

It's easy to look to the company, your upline, your group, or just bad luck when your business stumbles or falters. But the moment you do so, you relinquish control. When problems arise or your strategy isn't going according to plan, you have an opportunity to become stronger and develop new skills—skills that you can pass on to your recruits when they strike trouble.

Refuse to allow yourself to be derailed by outside influences. Only you can drive your business through ups and downs, triumphs and tears. You may have personal distractions to deal with. But you have set your goals, and you owe it to yourself to do whatever it takes to achieve them, no matter what happens along the way. Big dreams are worth making big sacrifices for.

Besides, where's the adventure in a journey with no surprises? Where's the opportunity to learn and grow when you overcome roadblocks that arose when you least expected them to?

Have the courage to make bold decisions, take action, review the consequences of your actions, and make more decisions. Decide, act, review; decide, act, review; . . .

When you accept that "If it's to be, it's up to me," you gain awesome power over your future.

WORKSHEET **SIX**: TAKE CHARGE

Before you go any further, make sure you can answer "Yes" to these five questions:

1. Am I ready to accept responsibility for my own future?

2. Am I realistic about the challenges I will face?

3. Do I understand that my chances of success increase with every person I recruit?

4. Am I willing to focus on what I have to do to succeed, not on what my corporate partner, recruits, or upline should be doing?

5. Am I willing to do whatever it takes to reach my destination?

Work the Hours

MY NEIGHBOR STEVE IS AN ENTHUSIAST. So when he started a network marketing business, I had never seen anyone so excited about the company with which he had signed, the groundbreaking products he now represented, and the success he was going to achieve. Determined to learn all he could about the business, Steve attended training, read the books, built an impressive library of tapes, and traveled great distances to attend seminars. The business consumed all his time and his thoughts.

Less than six months later, Steve told me he had quit the business. He sounded disappointed, disillusioned, and more than a little bitter about his network marketing experience. When we talked, it didn't take long to see what went wrong. Steve had invested six months learning the theory of the business, but very little time putting his knowledge to work.

As Steve talked out his frustration, it became clear that

he had not made nearly enough calls, or set up nearly enough appointments. When he did make an appointment, he often failed to make the sale. Instead of doing more calls, and more presentations, he went looking for more answers.

The one lesson that eluded Steve was a basic principle of network marketing: *The system works if you do.* At first you do more than you get paid for, but then you get paid for more than you do. That's what residual income means. It's income that keeps coming after you have done the work. But first you have to do the groundwork.

Think of an oil field. You know there's oil out there somewhere, but nothing is going to happen until you drill holes. Some will be dry, some will strike oil, and some will tap rich veins. The more holes you drill, the better your chances of striking oil. Once you have tapped a rich vein, the oil keeps pumping as long as you maintain the pumps.

It's the same in this business. There are no easy answers, magic formulas, or insider secrets to reveal. The number of hours you invest working your business will determine what you achieve and how quickly you achieve it.

You will gain knowledge, support, and inspiration from training, manuals, conference calls, and company meetings, but you won't build a business from theory. You will master the skills only through practice. The way to learn to play the guitar . . . is to play the guitar.

This business is simple, but it's not easy. That's why the rewards are high for those who succeed. Commit action time to your business and the results will follow.

Practice makes perfect. When you're working, note what works and what doesn't, make the necessary adjustments, and keep working. Small improvements every day add up to significant improvements over time.

The single greatest reason people fail in network marketing is that they do not put in the hours. Industry statistics show that of the fifty-four million people currently involved, the majority spend less than five hours a week working the business. No surprises here why most do not achieve their dreams.

You can be different. Work every day without exception, and work as many hours as you can. Industry research clearly shows that people who work their business consistently have significantly higher incomes than those who work erratic hours. Make daily lists, and work steadily through them. Work the phone, work the Internet, work the room, and work your community. The more people you connect with, the greater your chance of success.

Take your business seriously. Allocate specific times to work, and refuse to allow anything or anyone to intrude on that time. Just because you don't have to clock in doesn't mean you can take it easy. Cheat on your hours and you only cheat yourself. If you feel yourself flagging, take a closer look at the goals you sprinkled around the house to remind yourself what you are working for.

We all have different body clocks, but mornings are when most of us are fresh. Don't waste your most productive time pushing paper around a table. Start each day with a *Power Hour* working the key aspect of your business—making calls! You'll feel energized for the rest of the day, knowing you have dealt with your most important task.

Whatever happens, don't put off doing what you must do to achieve your goals. Activity leads to results, and results lead to rewards.

Procrastination is a fast pass to failure. When we delay important tasks, we don't forget them. We carry them around with us and, as the day draws on, the burden becomes heavier. Even a small load will start to feel heavy after an hour or two (try holding a small glass of water for more than an hour and see how quickly your arm aches). By tackling the tough jobs first, you will feel lighter for the rest of the day.

★ ★ ★ ★ ★ ★

Have you noticed that busy people always seems to find time for the important tasks? It's because they put such a high value on their time they don't waste it. Here are a few tricks that will help you maximize every minute:

❑ Keep your workspace uncluttered, so you're not sifting through a mountain of paper to find the one piece you want.

❑ Prepare recruiting packs and hostess packs in bulk.

❑ Unload some of your time-consuming tasks onto family members. Tell them, "Share the benefits, share the work."

❑ Put an egg timer by the phone and use it. Learn to say, "I wish we could chat longer, but I'd better get back to work," or "I know you are busy, so I won't keep you," when a call drags on.

❑ Prepare your To-Do list the night before and make sure you include phone numbers, to save time the next day. Stick to the list.

❑ Map your day before you set out, to avoid backtracking, side trips, or double ups; for example, make deliveries, post mail, and collect supplies on the way to an appointment.

❑ Carpool with your neighbors to ferry the kids to school and sports.

❑ Keep a permanent shopping list on the refrigerator to avoid unnecessary trips to the market. Encourage the family to add to it.

❑ Record your favorite television programs and fast-forward through the recaps, credits, and commercials. You'll cut a one-hour program nearly in half.

❑ Buy stamps, stationery, groceries, and other supplies in bulk.

❑ Set up automatic payments for your bills.

❑ Shop with other direct sellers, or shop on the Internet rather than at the mall.

❑ Use retailers who deliver.

❑ Check e-mails only once or twice a day.

❑ Put a junk-mail filter on your e-mail in-box.

❑ Attend to a task when you first think of it.

❑ Don't flit from task to task. Finish what you start.

Don't gamble with your future. Make sure you are among the hundreds of thousands of network marketers who make their dreams come true by working the hours.

WORKSHEET S E V E N : WORK THE HOURS

1. Set specific hours to work your business, separating productive time (i.e., appointments, interviews, prospecting) from administrative time.

2. Add up the hours you have allocated and ask, "Are my goals realistic in light of the time I have allowed?"

3. If you answered "Yes," you are in business. If not, find more time or revisit your goals (you will have plenty of time to work on lowering your golf handicap when your business is up and running). Ask yourself, "What can I delegate or set aside to make more time?"

4. Work the hours you have allocated. A cancelled appointment isn't a "get-out-of-work-free" card. Use the gap to make more calls.

5. Create time by cutting out waste. Use my suggestions or find your own time savers. If you can find an extra hour a day, you will have 365 hours in a year, or the equivalent of ten extra weeks of the average workweek, to invest.

I will create time by:

    a. _____

    b. _____

    c. _____

    d. _____

    e. _____

STEP
eight

Master Six Core Skills

ONE OF THE BENEFITS of network marketing is simplicity. Master three core skills and you are well on your way to success. Master three more and there's no ceiling on what you can achieve.

Imagine a toolbox. Inside, there are six tools to help you build a network marketing business: three basic tools for the simple tasks and three for the slightly more complex ones. The sooner you master each tool, the sooner you will get results.

Let's start with the basics.

1. *Scheduling.* Your planner is the only indicator of your business. A planner full of bookings and appointments means your business is in good shape. An empty page means your business is in jeopardy.

2. *Selling.* Your monthly check will depend on how much product you, and the people you recruit, sell.

3. *Recruiting.* Your business opportunity is your flagship product, and you won't succeed until you learn to promote it effectively.

Now we come to three advanced tools that will help you realize your most ambitious goals:

4. *Building Relationships.* One-off sales and chance en-counters will not build a strong business. If you are con-stantly working to find new customers and prospects, you will burn out before your business is secure.

5. *Mentoring.* Your success will ultimately depend on the success of the people you recruit. Although you are not re-sponsible for their success, you are responsible for the quality of support you give them.

6. *Managing.* Chaos does not make for a successful busi-ness. As your business grows, you will be juggling more than a few balls. You want to drop as few as possible.

There are only six tools, and you must master all of them. If you don't learn to schedule, it won't matter how good a salesperson you are, because you will have no ap-pointments. If you don't sell product and the people you recruit do not sell product, your check will hardly be worth cashing. You can't be a mentor without people in your down-line. Businesses don't run themselves.

As I cover each of these tools in subsequent chapters, remember that there is no better place to learn how to use each one than on the job.

No one will expect you to be perfect at the beginning. Don't be afraid to tell people that you are learning. They will appreciate your candor, and they may be encouraged to follow your lead when they see you don't have to know it all to get started.

Ask yourself:

1. Which of the tools have I mastered?

    ⋆ *Scheduling*: Let your planner answer this one for you.

    ⋆ *Recruiting*: Am I targeting and signing new recruits consistently?

    ⋆ *Selling*: How close am I to the average sale per customer for my products?

    ⋆ *Building Relationships*: Is my circle of friends and associates widening?

    ⋆ *Mentoring*: Do the people I recruit remain active longer than six to twelve weeks? Are they productive?

    ⋆ *Managing*: Am I in control of my business?

2. Which tools do I need to spend more time mastering?

    _____

    _____

3. Which tool needs my attention first?

    _____

    _____

Honor Your Planner

YOUR PLANNER DOES NOT BELONG HIDDEN in your briefcase or tucked away in your office. Keep it with you at all times, and keep it open so you can check the status of your business at a glance, based on how many appointments you have. If you don't have appointments you don't have a business.

Your first, and most important, task is to schedule appointments. Appointments won't materialize from nowhere. You have to make them. But first you have to set the times you will work.

Decide how many product demonstrations, parties, or business presentations you will do, and slot the times into your planner a month ahead. Use a highlighter pen or colored sticker to mark the time you have allocated so the blank spaces will jump out at you.

Now you are open for business. All you have to do is find names and contact details to complete each time slot.

The only way to fill these slots is to talk to people. In person, by phone, or by e-mail. Not everyone will say "Yes," so be prepared to make lots of calls. A one-in-ten response may be realistic if you are a novice, so count on making twenty calls a day to get two appointments.

If you get a better response, keep calling. Overbooking will buffer you against cancellations. Airlines and hotels know that booking capacity at 120 percent will cover cancellations and no-shows. You will find the same approach works for you. If you plan to do two shows a week, book three.

Monitor your planner daily to ensure you are fully booked at least two weeks ahead, and have a back-up plan for postponements. You have to fill the gaps unless you are prepared to let go of your dreams.

If your back-up plan fails and you find yourself with an empty slot in your planner, use the time to make more calls, or create an appointment on the spot. With a little ingenuity, you can always find someone to talk to—the salesperson at your favorite clothing store, the server at your local restaurant, your realtor, or the person working out beside you at the gym. Wondering how you can start a conversation cold? Get them talking about themselves and they'll ask about you (if they don't they are probably not good prospects anyway).

Accept that some appointments come easily and others take more effort. If you maintain an optimistic mind-set, opportunities will open up. Don't be timid. You are not trying to close the sale; you are simply asking for an opportunity to demonstrate your products, or discuss the business. There will never be a better time to set appointments than when you're sitting face-to-face across the table. If you're a party planner, you have a captive audience. However hard you have to work at a future booking, it will still be easier than a cold call the next morning.

Add to your network list every day, so you always have a pool of people to contact. You will be surprised how many people you meet, or hear about, when you commit to adding to the list daily.

You will find it easier to make appointments with people who know you, like you, and respect you. That's the number one reason you should service your customers regularly and stay in touch with everyone you meet. Don't be shy about asking for referrals, and reward those who offer them. Product, a discount, or a voucher redeemable off a future purchase all make inexpensive "thank you" gifts for an introduction. Every person you meet is potentially a link to many more. That's why it's called network marketing.

Never resort to tricks or fast-talk to get an appointment. If you are not proud of and excited at what you are offering, how can you expect others to be? Always be up front and enthusiastic: "I'm calling on business. Do you have a moment to talk?"

Have a positive reason why you are calling: "I called you because . . ."

Prospects will appreciate the compliment, respect your candor, and warm to your enthusiasm.

Resist the temptation to overexplain. Use phone calls to strengthen your relationship with your prospects, learn what you can about their circumstances, and confirm a time and place for the appointment. If it's a sale you are after, you may want to know what brands they currently use, and why. If you are aiming for a business appointment, you will be looking for a reason why they may need more money or a change of job.

Don't overwhelm your prospect. Ask questions and listen to the answers to find common ground, and why your product or business will improve her life. If you talk too much and listen too little you will be pushing uphill. Relax. You won't get the appointment if you've told the prospect all she needs to know over the phone, or if you talk at her instead of with her.

Don't allow yourself to be unnerved by rejections. You don't see retailers shutting up shop every time someone says, "Just looking, thanks," or walks out without buying. You don't see doctors closing down their practice because of a cancelled appointment. If you are hearing, "No thanks" too often, try a fresh approach.

It takes discipline to make twenty calls day after day. But this is how you build your business, and you have to do it until you are creating enough leads from the people you meet in the course of your day. Remind yourself that keeping your planner full is the hardest part of the business. Master the art of scheduling, keep your planner full, and you will be well over halfway toward achieving your goals.

. . . .
WORKSHEET **N I N E**: HONOR YOUR PLANNER
. . . .

1. Review and update your network list now.

2. Commit to adding at least one name to your list every day, more if you can.

3. Mark out your planner and make sure appointment times jump out at you.

4. Block out your daily *Power Hour*. If you need encouragement, put twenty small objects, such as marbles or coins, in a dish, and transfer one to another dish after each call.

5. Schedule appointments as soon as possible. The farther out they are, the more you risk a cancellation or postponement.

6. Commit to calling until your planner is full; then call some more. Think how good it will feel to say, "I'm booked solid this week [month], but how about early next week [month]?"

7. Check your planner every morning so you know exactly what times you must fill over the next two weeks.

STEP
ten

Sell, Don't Tell

THE FOUNDATION OF NETWORK MARKETING IS SALES.
No one gets paid until product moves. Your personal sales generate income as you build your business, and they set an example for your recruits to follow. The higher the total sales of your group, the higher your monthly check will be.

Start by becoming your own best customer. First, you will have no credibility if you expect others to buy your products when you are not buying them. Why should I get excited about your products if you're not? Second, there is no substitute for firsthand experience and personal endorsement of your products. It's your personal story that people will respond to, not a long list of features and benefits.

Building a loyal base of customers who use your products will guarantee you a steady income. Look for lifetime customers, not a quick sale, and you will be on your way to creating residual income.

If you belong to one of the growing number of companies that ship for you, or that offer an auto-ship program (where orders are shipped and charged direct from the company on a regular cycle), take advantage of it. But stay in touch. If you lose contact you lose future sales and you lose a potential recruit.

Any sales transaction with integrity should involve four actions:

1. *Start a relationship with your customer.* The stronger the ties you build with your customer, the more likely it is that you will make the sale, and many more for years to come. Don't fall into the "one-size-fits-all" trap. Each customer is unique, with different needs, interests, and ambitions that will help you identify the products from which he or she will benefit most. Every sale should start, and finish, with listening. Everyone loves talking about himself or herself, and your customer will enjoy telling you what you need to know to move to the second step.

2. *Show your customers how your product will make their life better.* In this age of instant gratification most of us are looking for products that offer simple solutions—to help us look a little younger or a little more attractive, to feel better or have more energy, to lose weight, to save money, to reduce stress, or to cancel out our bad habits. Don't complicate matters by telling your customers more than they need to know to buy. Find out what their issues are and show them how your product will make them right.

Keep the focus strictly on your customer. The data provided by your company will help if your customer asks for more detail. But few will. A volley of information is more likely to confuse or even alienate your customers than convince them to buy your product.

3. *Close the sale.* When you close, move confidently. Reassure hesitators with your belief in the product.

"My energy levels went from a 2 to a 10 after I started taking this supplement. It made a huge difference in how I felt."

"Your skin will feel softer. I noticed the difference almost immediately and my friends noticed too. I was getting lots of compliments about how great I was looking."

"As soon as you switch it on, your family will begin breathing cleaner air. My wife's cat allergy disappeared practically overnight."

"My kids love the taste of these rubs and I love the fact they're free of chemicals. It's a real win-win product."

"Knowing I had access to legal representation if and when I needed it took a huge load off my mind."

"My long-distance calls cost less than half what I used to pay. I save at least $20 a week and I no longer worry about how long I talk."

Reinforce your confidence in your products with the "top down" close. It's harder to climb up a slope than come down and it's the same with selling. Here's how it works:

Make your premium offer first—the deluxe program or top-of-the-line model. You are complimenting your customers when you assume they can afford the best. Start by saying, "If you want the best (or fastest) results, this is what I recommend."

If they demur, you can say, "If you prefer to build gradually, I recommend you start with these."

Again, if they do not want to spend that much, you can say, "Many of my customers start with this and upgrade from there."

At this point, stop talking. Silence gives your customer space to think and come to a decision. You may talk yourself out of a sale by applying pressure or talking while he is trying to decide. If you have to persuade your customer, you didn't do it right.

4. *Follow up to ensure that you have a satisfied customer.* Never lose sight of the fact that you are looking for lifetime customers. Make sure you make your customers feel good, whatever decision they make. Always promise that you will be calling to see how they enjoy their product, and/or keep them informed about upcoming promotions. It is much easier to say, "I promised to call to check how you are enjoying your products," than to have to explain why you are calling. If you don't make the sale say, "I'll stay in touch, if that's okay with you." When you have permission to call, you are more likely to make the call, and make it confidently.

Keep brief notes on each customer, so you don't have to search your memory bank each time you call. "How are you today?" is a pretty shallow opener.

★ ★ ★ ★ ★ ★

Does this all seem very basic? If it does, it's because it is. Network marketing works from repeat business earned through quality products, excellent service, and ongoing relationships.

Yet, most salespeople forget their training when they are face-to-face with customers and after a halfhearted attempt to show genuine interest barrage them with sales speak. Aaargh . . . !

Do it right, and you will soon see your skill and professionalism reflected in your sales.

. . . .
WORKSHEET **T E N** : SELL, DON'T TELL
. . . .

1. Make sure you have a compelling answer to the question, "What is special about your products?" For exam-

ple, if you are marketing weight loss products, say, "I've always been a bit of a fast-food junkie and could never keep to a diet. But when I discovered these delicious shakes and snack bars I lost five pounds in the first two weeks."

What is so special about your products? Write your answer here:

_____

_____

_____

_____

_____

_____

2. Practice selling your products to friends, family, or team members. Ask them for feedback (the best feedback will be when they buy what you're selling).

3. After a few practice runs, step back and decide how you are going to increase your selling skills:

I will start _____

I will stop _____

I will remember to _____

4. Work out how you are going to handle your follow-up calls.

_____

_____

_____

5. Devise a simple system to maintain your customer records.

_____

_____

_____

eleven

Radiate Positive Energy

TO BUILD A QUALITY BUSINESS you need quality people. The best way to attract quality people is to become a live advertisement for your business.

We are attracted to people who have the qualities we wish we had, so the image you project will determine how others respond to you. First impressions are especially important when you are constantly reaching out to new people.

Each time you walk out your door, you create a positive or negative impression.

Before you step out, imagine you have to pass a hat stand. Imagine three hats hanging on pegs, waiting for you to put them on. Each hat is a vivid color.

These imaginary hats will remind you to project the three characteristics of successful network marketers, and increase your chances of attracting high-caliber people.

The first hat is red.

Red signifies confidence and success. You will stand out in the crowd in red so always carry yourself as if you were wearing the red hat.

But worn alone, the red hat can be overpowering. You want people to notice you, but also to warm to you.

You need the yellow hat.

The yellow hat casts an aura of warmth and happiness. It says that you like people and expect them to like you, that you enjoy what you do and that you are fun to be around. Happiness is contagious. If you project yourself as if you are wearing the yellow hat, people will be drawn toward you.

But that's not enough. Many rising stars in this industry reach a plateau in their business because they neglect the third hat.

The third hat is blue.

The blue hat projects the qualities of the highest leaders. The blue hat is calm and relaxed. It tells the world that you live a balanced life. Forgetting the blue hat will send a signal that you are paying too high a price for your success.

Rushing, driving or talking too fast, arriving late or breathless for appointments, not maintaining eye contact, losing your cool at minor upsets, being a poor listener, and forgetting names are just a few signs that the blue hat is missing.

We all want to be successful. But if the price is too high, people will turn away. When you project stress, pressure, and tension, potential recruits will think, "Thanks, but no thanks."

Slow down, allow for the unexpected, and give people your full attention. When you find yourself rushing, take a deep breath and remember your blue hat.

You are not only marketing an income opportunity. You are marketing quality of life. To do so you have to embody the qualities of someone enjoying quality of life. Financial success without balance is a hollow victory.

Not everything will go your way all the time. Learn to

love the business for all that it brings and accept good times and bad as two sides of the same coin. Whatever challenges you are experiencing, project an aura of confidence, happiness, and calm. Your charisma will soon attract the people who will help you build a dynamic business.

WORKSHEET ELEVEN: RADIATE POSITIVE ENERGY

1. Take an honest look at the image you project. What areas are working for you?

_____

_____

2. What areas are not working for you?

_____

_____

3. What steps will you take to improve your image?

I will start

_____

_____

I will stop

_____

_____

I will remember

_____

_____

I will always

_____

_____

I will never

_____

_____

4. Begin your transformation into the person you aspire to become by making one change. It's okay to be a work in progress.

twelve

Focus on Relationships

YOU WILL HAVE NOTICED that I talk a lot about relationships. That's because when you take away the relationship aspect of network marketing there is nothing left to distinguish you from any other retailer, direct marketer, or online seller.

Your products may be superb, but only the most naïve marketer believes that her product is the only quality product on the market.

Your company may be amazing, with a to-die-for compensation plan, brilliant incentives, and staff who will go to the ends of the earth to serve you, but there are other companies out there with great plans, incentives, and staff.

Your training programs and support systems may be state-of-the-art. But with the fast-moving advances in technology, anyone can mimic those advances as fast as they are developed. The only thing that cannot be copied, or imitated, is the relationship you build with others.

It takes five times the effort and energy to find a new customer or replace someone in your downline than to keep the one you have. So it will come as no surprise that the top tier of achievers spend most of their time developing relationships with their downline, whereas their less-successful counterparts are forever working to replace people who are leaving.

Relationships need both quantity and quality of contact to develop.

Start with your customers. It takes discipline to follow up all sales with a "satisfaction" call, and to service your customers regularly. But in the long run, you will save time because you will not be forever chasing new business, and you'll increase your chances of a customer becoming a recruit.

The wider you spread your net, the better your chances of finding customers and recruits. Nurture relationships with neighbors, colleagues, suppliers, and others within your community. The more people you know, the better your chances of finding potential recruits, and sparing yourself the painstaking process of cold calling or scattering flyers about town.

Joining a gym or service club, or taking an adult education class, will widen your circle of contacts, as will doing volunteer work in your community. When you give, you gain respect in return. The more people respect you, the more open they will be to your approach. The messenger carries more weight than the message.

We like people who like us, and show genuine interest in us. Put your ego aside and give the people you meet your complete attention. Maintain eye contact, and don't allow yourself to be distracted. Learn to ask questions and listen to and remember the answers, so when you next meet you will have meaningful conversations instead of superficial small chat.

If all this does not come naturally, work at it. Look for common threads—family, friends, interests, work, and local issues. Bonds will build faster and stronger when you find interests or beliefs in common.

When you are asked a question, answer it, and direct the conversation back with another question. Practice this over and over until it becomes second nature.

Keep records of people you meet. Set aside a few minutes at the end of each day to update your contact files and send e-mails to connect with your contacts. If you rely on scraps of paper and hastily scribbled notes, you will most likely lose valuable leads. If you are working smart, you will have already established a reason to make contact—the title of a book, an interesting article or website that came up naturally in conversation.

★ ★ ★ ★ ★ ★

As you build your organization, your ability to build relationships with the people who paid you the compliment of joining you will be a key factor in your success. Never be so busy finding new people that you neglect those already in your group.

As your downline grows, you will find yourself working with a mix of personalities. Recognize that everyone has different goals, styles, and viewpoints. Great businesses are built on a diversity of skills and experiences.

You will generate loyalty by offering the best training and support you can, based on each person's circumstances and needs. Small gestures—such as promptly returning calls, remembering special occasions, and acknowledging milestones—can make a big difference. Turning off your cell phone when you are with others shows you respect their time.

Your new recruits need close contact as they transition from reliance to independence. The bond you build with new people may stop them from walking away before they have given their business a fair chance of succeeding.

Focusing on new people and those who make the biggest

contribution is sound business sense, but it takes little effort to make everyone feel valued. People stay where they feel important and appreciated.

As your business grows, you will have increasing pressures on your time. Set an example by building strong relationships with your first levels. Your example will encourage them to build strong relationships with the people they recruit right down the line.

You want everyone to feel the pride that comes with belonging to an organization with a genuine commitment to helping people achieve their personal goals.

No matter how talented you are as a leader, people will enter and leave your business all the time. How you respond when they leave will speak volumes about you. Never be too preoccupied with the future that you forget to thank them for their contribution and let them know they will always be welcome back.

WORKSHEET **TWELVE**: FOCUS ON RELATIONSHIPS

Write down your answers to the following questions:

1. "What must I do to increase contact with my customers?"

_____

_____

_____

2. "How can I build stronger bonds within my community?"

_____

_____

_____

3. "How can I build closer relationships within my group?"

_____

_____

_____

thirteen

Keep It Simple

THE PATH TO FAILURE IS PAVED WITH DETAIL. I've lost count of how many times I've watched from the sidelines as customers lost interest during a sales presentation or prospects switched off halfway through a lecture on the company's compensation plan.

Make "keeping it simple" a driving philosophy throughout your business. Start with the way you market your products and business opportunity.

Words will not convince people to buy your product or get excited about your business. The fewer words you use, the more time you will have to spend on what really counts—getting to know prospects, finding out what they want, and showing them how you can make it happen.

The average commercial on television is thirty seconds. Why? Because that's what works! Any shorter and the advertiser will struggle to make the point; any longer and the viewer will start flicking channels.

How do advertisers create commercials that hit home in such a short time frame? The same way you will create commercials for your business. By focusing on *simplicity* and *impact*.

Decide what you want to say and edit your words to bring out the magic. It's not what you leave in, but what you leave out that counts, unless you want to be talking to minds that are closed to incoming traffic.

When you overexplain your products, you insult your customers' intelligence. If they want to know more they will ask, and they will listen more intently because it interests them. Party planners will find that sales and bookings flow from parties that are lively, informative, and interactive. Too much information will guarantee a stodgy, uninspiring event.

Giving out too much information when you first approach business prospects invites them to make a decision on the spot. Your chance to make a planned presentation, based on their specific interests and circumstances, goes up in smoke.

If words will not convince people to get excited about your business, neither will time.

Keep your business presentations short, ideally no more than forty minutes. Spend the first third getting to know your prospect, the next third sharing the key points of your business based on what you learned. Spend the last third answering questions and deciding on the next move: signing the agreement, scheduling another meeting with a spouse, giving your prospect literature to read and agreeing to follow up the next day, or passing.

Assume that everyone is busy. Always let your prospects know how long the appointment will take. Never exceed that time. People will relax when you respect their space and schedule. Full-time workers will be more willing to meet with you if they know they can meet for a chat over a sandwich and return to work within a one-hour lunch break. You can always schedule a second meeting.

Apply the same discipline to opportunity nights or business seminars. Plan to take no more than ninety minutes from start to finish. Greet guests as they arrive and let them know you appreciate the time they have taken to learn about the business. Let your starter kit, recruiting literature, and key products work for you by displaying them where guests can look, read, and touch.

Keep the formal part short and stimulating, leaving time for interaction. Overrun your time and your guests will stampede toward the exit the first chance they get. Finish talking while they are still intrigued . . . and you'll get your chance to close the deal.

Although it takes work and discipline to make things simple, your efforts will pay dividends when you get results.

· ·
WORKSHEET **T H I R T E E N** : KEEP IT SIMPLE
· ·

1. Describe your business in fifty to one hundred words. If it's too wordy, look for what you can edit out.

_____

_____

_____

_____

_____

_____

2. Now practice your delivery, as if you are talking to an interested prospect. Do you sound natural? Do the words flow? Are they persuasive? Can you say what you want to say in thirty to sixty seconds?

3. Following the same format, create a variety of "commercials" for your business, appealing to a range of personalities, circumstances, and ambitions, such as income, products, incentives, training, support, and your personal experiences.

4. Map out and rehearse a business appointment with a friend. Ask for his or her feedback on areas that seem superfluous, repetitious, dull, or confusing.

5. If you are taking part in a business seminar, have a dress rehearsal. If you blow the actual performance you may never have a chance at those prospects again (unless you have the chutzpah to call and say, "Remember the dog's dinner I made out of my first presentation to you?").

fourteen

Become an Effective Communicator

THERE ARE FEW BORN COMMUNICATORS. Most of us have to work at developing our communication skills.

The best communicators understand that people are incredibly self-centered. Need convincing that this is true? Picture what happens when you are shown a photo taken with family or friends. You immediately scan the photo for yourself! No matter how lofty our dreams to be selfless are, self-centeredness is a fact of human nature.

It follows that people will respond to you when you talk about them. Before you fall into the salesman's chat trap, learn to ask questions and personalize your message.

We think at six times the rate we read, speak, or listen. That leaves a lot of time for minds to wander as you speak. Although it's easier to repeat a sales patter than to adapt your approach to suit each person, when you talk about things that do not engage your target, he will most likely be filling his time thinking about something else entirely.

Your prospects will come from different backgrounds and will have different experiences and perceptions. They will filter everything you say through the beliefs and prejudices they have formed throughout their lives. You can't expect your message to hit home if you are taking random shots.

Our attention spans are getting shorter by the day as more and more "voices" compete to capture our interest. Researchers claim that the average person is subjected to over 5,000 messages a day. It makes sense not to add to the overload.

When you speak less, you have to make every word matter. Black and white tells; color sells. Color your conversations and presentations with stories and anecdotes. Bring your products and business opportunity to life with personal experiences and compelling examples.

Spare your listener hype and myths. Not only is it unethical to talk up your business, but if you tell a recruit she can make $20,000 a month within six months you are also going to have one disillusioned puppy on your hands when it doesn't happen. And the chances are high that your unhappy recruit will spread the word.

Avoid industry jargon, especially when you are prospecting or interviewing. Abbreviations like *IBO, PV,* and *BV,* or words like *upline, downline, width, depth,* and *residual income* can confuse and even alienate newcomers to the business. Use everyday language your customers, prospects, and raw recruits can relate to. If you are talking about new concepts, check with your listeners by asking, "Does this make sense?" or "Am I explaining this well enough?"

A significant portion of communication is visual. When we like what we see we are predisposed to like the message. Before you even open your mouth, your audience is deciding how credible you are and how interested they are in what you have to say.

If your appearance is shabby it will pay you to scrub up before you start promoting your business. You are investing in your business's greatest asset. If money is tight, buy less and buy quality (as a young mother I ran the first six months of my business with one suit).

If you are selling weight-loss products, try to look like a poster child for the product, or at least have a stack of "before" and "after" photos to show you are making progress. It's not just about your personal appearance. Turn up in a scruffy car, or with battered demonstration stock, and you deserve the cool reception you will most likely get.

The quality of your voice also makes a strong impression. Your timbre, pace, and volume will convey confidence and credibility or insecurity and insincerity. Voice quality can be learned, and it will pay dividends if you fix problems you may have. It's okay to be nervous but there's no excuse for being flat.

Our eyes are the mirrors to our thoughts. Maintaining eye contact not only flatters your audience, because you are talking directly with her, but it enables you to tell when your listener's interest is waning. When you see it happening, change your pace, tell a story, or ask a question to win back her attention. There is often a fine line between a "Yes" and a "No" decision. Ignore your prospect's perspective, override her concerns, or let her mind wander and you diminish your chances of hearing that magnificent question, "How soon can I start?"

Communication is a fundamental skill in any people business. You will not reach your peak without becoming an effective communicator. If you lack confidence, have difficulty with technical aspects of communication, or want to fine-tune your presentations, get outside help. Many excellent courses on public speaking are available, and organizations such as Toastmasters can help you become a better communicator.

. . . .
WORKSHEET **FOURTEEN**:
BECOME AN EFFECTIVE COMMUNICATOR
. . . .

1. Do you need outside help to improve your speaking skills? If the answer is "Yes," register for a course or join Toastmasters. Not sure? You probably need help, so join Toastmasters anyway, and use it as an opportunity to develop and fine-tune your presentations.

2. Practice this simple three-question rule at home and at work:
   a. Ask a question.
   b. Listen carefully to the answer; then ask another.
   c. Then ask another *before* you start talking.

3. Suppress the urge to interrupt a speaker, or think about your answer before he finishes speaking. If you are struggling to eliminate this bad habit, count to three before you open your mouth.

4. Practice key presentations in the car, while exercising, or in front of a mirror. Rehearse them over and over and over until you are happy with how you sound.

5. Don't cling to presentations that are not working for you. If you are not getting results, change your message or change the way you deliver it.

fifteen

Keep Finding New People

THE ONLY WAY TO GROW YOUR BUSINESS is to consistently introduce fresh faces. The day you stop introducing new people is the day your business will start sliding backward.

New people will add to your sales volume and, if you inspire them, introduce more new people. They will bring new ideas, excitement, energy, and momentum, and they will be living proof to everyone in your group that people want to join the business.

A strong business needs both width (people you personally recruit) and depth (people recruited by the people you recruit). There is no better way to get your people recruiting than to introduce a parade of new people yourself.

Avoid making these costly mistakes:

* Relying on the people already in your downline to carry your business

★ Relying on the people you recruit to bring people into your business

In an ideal world, it would be wonderful if both these things worked. But when you rely on others you abdicate responsibility for the success of your business to them. This makes no sense.

The First Rule of Recruiting

The first rule of recruiting is *numbers*. Why? There is security in numbers. People will come and go. Some will stay a long time, others a short time. Some people will perform higher, and others lower, than you expect. And some will not perform at all, in spite of your best efforts. Even good performers may leave suddenly and take a big chunk of your sales volume with them.

If you recruit only a small number of people you will be at the mercy of their individual performances. The more people you have in your group, especially first levels, the more invincible you will be.

The Second Rule of Recruiting

The second rule of recruiting is *balance*. Balance comes from having enough personal recruits to insure you against the stellar performance of one person (leg) of your business. Don't rely on one or two "stars" to produce your volume. Discovering a stellar performer in your downline can be an intoxicating experience. Your results soar, and you bask in the recognition and rewards that follow. You spend so much time nurturing your star that you neglect your own sales and recruiting. Suddenly, the bubble bursts. Your shining star breaks away (elevates to a higher rank) and your income from the breakaway group may stop, or drop significantly, until you rebuild your personal group. Or, your shining star turns into a shooting star, exhibiting a flash of brilliance before disappearing forever.

Depend on one person to produce a disproportionate share of your results, and your business becomes vulnerable to the performance of that person.

Besides, the more breakaways you develop, the faster you will rise through the ranks to the top levels where the highest incomes are earned. Your chances of finding potential breakaways rises with every new person you recruit.

The Third Rule of Recruiting

The third rule of recruiting is to *look for people with the desire and the drive to move up the ranks quickly.* Think about where you are most likely to see stars.

You've got it—you're not going to find stars by looking earthward, but by lifting your sights high!

Outstanding leaders know the best way to build their businesses is to surround themselves with the best people they can find. Network marketing is no different. Set your sights on potential leaders. Start with people who are already successful at what they do. Look for bright sparks who have yet to reach their potential. When you look up, you will see stars.

Even if your prospect declines your offer, try to maintain contact. Circumstances and attitudes can change overnight. If you don't stay in touch, someone who is in the right place at the right time will reap the benefit of your preliminary work. This industry teems with successful network marketers who were approached, declined, and then subsequently joined under someone else—having never heard from the original person again. It pays to be patient and it pays to be persistent.

Broadening Your Reach

Prospect for recruits in the places that best fit your organization. Think: *Who would be interested in the business, why would they be interested, and how will I approach them?*

If your system is business oriented, plug into business and professional associations. Wellness centers, medical suites, fitness centers, and spas are a great fit for health products. If you are a party planner, fill your planner with demonstrations, classes, spas, and parties.

It's always easier to find people like ourselves. But the wider range of people you recruit the better. Look for people who bring fresh skills, attitudes, and experiences into the team, not just those you find easy to approach. The secret to a winning team is balance.

Broaden your reach by thinking outside the box. For example, parents may be the obvious choice for educational books, scrapbooking, and toys, but grandparents have checkbooks too (especially where grandkids are concerned). Grandparents also have the time to devote to a new business, a lifetime of skills and experience to share, and perhaps a pressing need to top up their 401K. When you consider that 90 percent of Americans never achieve financial independence, there is an enormous pool of potential prospects for your opportunity.

The point is not to restrict yourself. Anyone, anywhere, anytime is a good rule to follow. Think "Who?" and then, "Who else?" Your next recruit could be the server in your coffee shop, your dentist, your cleaner, a neighbor who collects the newspaper at the same time you do each morning, a fellow student in your communications class at the Adult Education Center, your son's teacher, or someone they refer you to. Always have your antenna up.

Never assume any prospect will not be interested. Hundreds of thousands of people from all walks of life join this industry every year to achieve financial freedom without risking capital, and without sacrificing family, friends, and leisure time. There is only one guaranteed way to lose a recruit, and that is not to ask.

Although your strategy should be to build your business with quality people, don't prejudge. Everyone deserves a chance. If it doesn't work out, the person will have risked nothing and lost nothing, except the opportunity to make money; work from home; learn new skills; become more confident; and have more time for leisure, traveling, and making new friends.

What have *you* lost? Nothing but a few minutes of your time. And that's only if you don't subscribe to the theory that we get better with practice.

Sow seeds everywhere, and nourish them with contact. Don't be in a rush or you will risk appearing overeager. Take time to get to know people, and always stay on the lookout for clues that may indicate an interest or a need.

If you understand the value of what you are offering, you will find it easier to approach people. When you approach people you believe are great candidates for the business, you are paying them a compliment. You are not trying to convince them to join you, but to tell them about the opportunity and offer your support if they decide to sign. If you approach prospects sensitively, they will be flattered, even if they pass on your offer.

WORKSHEET FIFTEEN: KEEP FINDING NEW PEOPLE

1. Are you adding to your network list every day?

2. If not, are you meeting enough people?

3. Are you talking to at least one person a day about the business?

4. If not, what do you have to do to meet more likely prospects?

5. Make a habit of asking these three simple questions:
   a. "Who will be interested in my business?"
   b. "Why would they be interested?"
   c. "How will I approach them?"

6. Make up six recruiting packs and take them with you wherever you go. An opportunity to give them out may present itself anywhere, anytime. Never have less than six ready to hand to prospects.

7. Ask, "Where will I find future leaders?" Position yourself where you are most likely to come into contact with motivated people.

sixteen

Become a Mentor

THERE ARE FEW MORE REWARDING ROLES in life than to be a mentor, and the catalyst for another person's success.

People will enter your business with a wide range of abilities and goals. The majority will always work this business on a casual basis. The collective sales of these small producers can produce significant volume.

A few are destined to become top performers. These perfect candidates for mentoring will identify themselves by their results. They are your future breakaways—leaders with the potential to inspire, motivate, train, and support their own people. The more breakaways you develop the greater your chance of long-term success.

Being a mentor takes energy and commitment. For the relationship to work, the commitment must be mutual. Focus your attention on performers who earn your support by what they do, not what they say. Don't be dazzled by someone who talks the talk until they show that they can also walk the talk.

Being new to the business should not stop you from becoming a mentor. Think of the relationship you have with your children. You don't profess to have all the answers but you care about them, and you know their strengths and what they can achieve. You share your knowledge and values with them, give them your full support, and allow them space to grow—mistakes and all.

If you run your business as you raise your kids, you will become a powerful mentor. Sharing your vision and experience, establishing expectations and guidelines based on the goals your stars set for themselves, and offering honest feedback and support along the way will empower them to reach their fullest potential.

Think about how you teach your kids to play board games. You teach them the rules and then take turns to move. When they make a wrong move, you suggest alternatives ones, until they become skilled players: *Your move, my move, your move, my move* . . .

Approach mentoring the same way. Your goal is for your recruits to become confident leaders who will, in turn, pass on their skills and experience to the people they recruit. If you do too much for them, or make too many allowances for nonperformance (remember that they set the goalposts), you are doing them no favors. Think, "Your move, my move, your move, my move . . ."

Mentoring can be time-consuming and it can be tempting to let your personal sales and recruiting activity slide while you focus on your protégé. But balancing your time between personal activity and coaching others makes business sense. Although you have taken on new responsibilities, if you stop doing the things that brought you to this point, you will stop growing. Besides, when the person you have mentored becomes the independent leader you knew she could be, it's time to mentor someone new. You won't find that person unless you maintain a flow of people into your business.

. . . .
WORKSHEET **SIXTEEN** : BECOME A MENTOR
. . . .

1. Ask, "What qualities would I look for in a mentor?" and model yourself on those qualities.

_____

_____

_____

_____

_____

_____

_____

2. List your best prospects for mentoring. If you don't have anyone yet, and you have recruited more than ten people, try raising your sights when you prospect. Ask, "Who would I love to have in my business?" and start by approaching them.

_____

_____

_____

_____

_____

_____

3. Before you begin any mentoring program make sure the recipient of your attention commits to a specific goal, and to the time necessary to achieve that goal.

4. Regularly review your mentoring program to ensure you are investing your time and effort in the people who produce results.

Embrace the Tools

**DO YOU HAVE TO INCORPORATE NEW TECHNOLO-
GIES** into your network marketing business?

Only if you want to succeed!

Most network marketing companies invest heavily in so-
phisticated technologies for their representatives. It makes
sense to take advantage of them.

Technology gives you a competitive edge over "traditional" businesses, which have become increasingly weighed
down by administrative costs, government regulations, and
unproductive staff. It allows you to run your business efficiently, and concentrate on the frontline activities that create
your income.

Let's start with the most basic of all: a sales transaction.
The Internet has transformed the way we shop. Each year
more than 40 million American households shop online,
spending over $120 billion. These statistics, however, don't

reflect the true power of the Internet. For every person who shops online, there are hundreds more who research products online before they buy.

The Internet makes it possible to send information to many people quickly and cheaply. It allows you to personalize bulk messages and to produce a regular schedule of fresh messages and follow-ups—everything you would do if only you "had more time."

When you send an e-mail newsletter out to your customers you can see who opened it. Calling them is much easier when you can say, "Did you see anything you liked in this month's specials?" Party planners can see who clicked on the link to party or host invitations. Your well-timed follow-up sales call could turn a "maybe I will/maybe I won't" into a party guest or host.

And what about keeping yourself abreast of news? New telephone technologies make participating in a telephone conference call or seminar an efficient way to learn new techniques, receive upcoming promotions and products, and hear company news firsthand.

Many companies offer teleconferencing, teleseminars (by phone), or Web conferencing (on your computer) at no cost to you, but even if you pay to participate, there are still enormous savings in time and travel costs compared to attending a meeting or conference.

Technology makes managing your business easier. When you have an Internet link to your corporate partner you can track results and spot instantly where to invest your time and energy. By monitoring your business on a weekly or even daily basis, you can provide instant recognition to those who are progressing and give tangible support to those who are struggling. It's like having an office in the corporate building—only better!

Behind the front line, there are many consumer-friendly computer programs to help you deal with your business and tax obligations efficiently, freeing you to concentrate on the activities that create your income.

High-tech tools, and the terms that describe them, may initially overwhelm you. A bewildering array of buzzwords has evolved to describe these new tools. Don't let words intimidate you. The engineers of these tools know that they have to be simple to use, or they won't sell. They are designed to make life easier for you.

The bottom line is that the Internet is your ultimate tool. It is your link to your corporation, your customers, your downline, and your upline. It enables you to develop a global business from your home office or kitchen table.

Developing an Internet strategy for your business will put you on an equal footing with your competitors.

Keep your website fresh and topical. It is your shop window and will work well for you if it is updated regularly with new products, tips, or information to keep customers interested.

If managing your own website is not your strong suit, look for ways your corporate partner can assist. If your corporation does not yet offer that support, you'll find help in the Yellow Pages. Or, you may need to look no further than your own family. One of our sons developed and manages my website (www.marychristensen.com); the other makes sure I am using the latest tools to help me communicate with my clients wherever I am. It's second nature to them and a huge support for me.

A word of caution. For all its advantages, the Internet can't perform miracles. Like any tool, it is designed to help you, not do the job for you. It has to be used in the right way, at the right time, and in the right place. It is not a substitute for personal contact. Nevertheless, taking advantage of all the tools that have been created to help you look after your customers and maintain your business will free you to concentrate on the person-to-person interaction that is the magic of network marketing.

WORKSHEET **SEVENTEEN**: EMBRACE THE TOOLS

1. Review all your corporate partner's resource materials. Are you tapping into everything that is available?

2. Are there any tools you don't understand? Who could explain them to you?

3. Is there more you can do to free up your time or manage your business more effectively?

eighteen

Keep Moving, Whatever Happens

MOMENTUM IS EVERYTHING. You cannot fail in network marketing if you keep moving. It's fine to set your own pace, based on your personal goals, abilities, and circumstances. This is not a race. There will always be people who progress faster and slower than you. Staying the distance to achieve your goals is what counts, however long it takes. The hare and the tortoise both crossed the finish line.

Sometimes you will progress faster than others. Other times you'll encounter unexpected roadblocks and have to backtrack, or take a detour or two. But if you set out with the certain knowledge of where you want to go, and the determination to do whatever it takes to get there, the only way you can fail is if you stop moving.

A mature business attitude is critical to success. You will

set yourself up to fail if you believe that things will always go your way, or if you feel discouraged when you progress at a slower pace than you planned. Every single step you take is a step toward your goals. Expect your journey to be challenging and you won't be disappointed when you encounter difficulties. You will find a way to keep moving, whatever happens.

Starting out is the easiest part of network marketing. The strength to keep moving when the going gets rough is the true test. Too many people in this industry give up after the first few bumps. Not you. Accept that the journey will have adrenaline-rushing dips and peaks. Every challenge you overcome will make you stronger and better equipped for the next one.

If you are serious about success, you cannot afford to let outside influences affect you. You have to believe:

* I cannot control what happens to me, but I *can* control whether I allow it to affect me.
* I cannot control what other people say, do, or think, but I *can* control my own thoughts, words, and actions.

Pointing the finger or making excuses will take you on a fast track to nowhere. Think of all the skills you have already mastered in life:

* How much effort did you put into learning to walk?
* How much effort did you put into learning to read?
* How long did it take you to learn to ride your bicycle?
* How many lessons did you take before you passed your driver's license test?
* How hard did you work to learn a second language?
* How quickly did you master basic computer skills?

★ How many hours did you study to pass an important exam?

It took masses of effort and energy to master skills you now take for granted. No doubt you had your share of failures, but imagine how your life would be if you had given up trying to walk because you took a few spills.

You will master the skills of network marketing, no matter how daunting it may seem after the end of the "honeymoon" period—when you look to your inner circle of family, friends, and acquaintances to see you through.

You will master the skills just as you mastered all the other skills you have acquired in life. And your life will be transformed because you stuck with it. As will the life of all the people you will bring into the business who find their niche in network marketing.

Only you can pull the brakes on your business. As Winston Churchill famously said, "Never give in, never give in, never give in."

. . . .
WORKSHEET **EIGHTEEN**: KEEP MOVING, WHATEVER HAPPENS
. . . .

1. Test your stamina with these questions:

"Am I willing to keep moving forward until I reach my goals?"

"Am I realistic about the challenges I may face on the way?"

"Am I willing to change myself when the need arises, rather than expect circumstances or others to change?"

2. Ask every potential leader the same questions before you agree to become his or her mentor.

3. When you encounter challenges, ask, "What is the best way for me to handle this situation?"

4. When your recruits come to you for help, encourage them to find their own solutions by asking, "What do you think is the best way to handle this situation?"

nineteen

Bend, Don't Break

ACHIEVERS IN ANY FIELD know how important it is to be flexible. A mountaineer expects that the climb will not be a straightforward ascent. He anticipates having to find a way around obstacles, or backtrack to find a safer path as he climbs to the peak. Any successful CEO understands the unpredictability of the markets and knows she must respond quickly and confidently when the need arises.

It's the same for you. You are not building your business in a vacuum, but in the real world, where you cannot control your environment.

When everything is firing, it's easy to feel unstoppable. Perhaps you are on target to move up a level in the compensation plan, earn a car, or achieve a trip to an international seminar.

Then, just when you thought nothing could go wrong, everything does. Someone you counted on lets you down. A promised sale doesn't come about. A hot prospect changes her mind at the eleventh hour.

It's natural to feel frustrated when your best-laid plans are thwarted. But the sooner you accept that it has happened, the sooner you can start doing whatever it takes to get back on track.

Birds constantly correct their path in flight. Changing weather conditions, the appearance of predators or prey, and the flight path of other birds may all call for a change of direction, position, or speed. And pilots, despite the most advanced navigation technologies, keep making adjustments to hold the airplane to its flight path.

It's the same in business. You have to keep correcting, correcting, and correcting to stay on course.

Nowhere will flexibility matter more than in your dealings with customers, prospects, and downline. Like all people businesses, network marketing can be volatile. Your people will have different aspirations. They will think and learn differently and respond to different stimuli. Where one person sees black, another will see white. Expecting everyone to think and act the same will inhibit your chances of success, as will trying to persuade others to understand your point of view instead of seeking to understand theirs.

Here's a sobering thought: Less than one tenth of one percent of all animal species that ever existed are still around today! The rest didn't adapt fast enough to a changing environment. When it comes to business, the odds are not much better. The average survival rate for new companies is estimated to be only about 20 percent by the fifth year of operation.

Being flexible is critical to survival. The more quickly we adapt to our ever-changing environment, the more we improve our odds of success.

If your strategy is not working, ask, "What am I doing, or not doing, right?"

When Plan A isn't working, you have to switch to Plan

B. If Plan B comes unstuck, develop Plan C. You won't solve a problem by continuing with the strategy that created it.

Review your goals regularly to ensure you are on track. Strategies can be amended and so can goals. There is little point in clinging to targets that are unrealistic. Many of network marketing's top achievers had at least one false start before they found the right gear.

WORKSHEET **N I N E T E E N** : BEND, DON'T BREAK

1. Cultivate a genuine curiosity about people to help you learn to understand and appreciate differing personality styles.

2. Always seek to understand the other person's point of view. Walk a few steps in his shoes before you rush to judgment.

3. Never become complacent. Keep reviewing, revising, and refreshing your strategy, based on the results you are getting.

4. Try not to carry baggage from one day to the next. Learn to draw a line under each day, and start the next day afresh.

5. Have the courage to make bold changes when your strategy is not working for you. You can't cross a chasm in two jumps.

6. Move quickly when responding to changing conditions. Even when things seem unjust, accept what happened and focus on your next move.

twenty

Manage Your Priorities

THERE WILL ALWAYS BE TWENTY-FOUR HOURS IN EACH DAY—no more, no less. Yet busy people make the best recruits, and busy people fill the top tier of this industry. Somehow, they find time to do what they want to do. Their secret? Understanding that they can't control time, but they can control how they use it. It's all about setting priorities.

When you plan your day, ask yourself three key questions:

1. "Will this help me make more bookings or appointments?"
2. "Will this help me recruit more people?"
3. "Will this help me make more sales?"

Although your goals may take years to accomplish, your activities should focus on the present: "What needs to be done now?"

If you spend your day rushing from task to task, chances are you have yet to learn to choose what's important and what's not. Time won't expand just because you have lots to do. You have to take time *from* one activity to give *to* another.

Successful people forgo small indulgences every day to bring their dreams to fruition. Learn to say "No" unless you are willing to sacrifice your dreams to someone else's agenda. There is no honor in being a martyr.

The hardest door to get through will always be your own. By practicing self-restraint, and by applying big doses of discipline to your day, you will be able to enjoy unforgettable experiences: company-recruited trips to exotic locations, money to spend on luxuries like no-expense-spared family vacations (and the time to enjoy them), a mortgage-free home, the best education for your children, the means to support your favorite charity, your dream car, or—the best of all—never having to worry about money again.

If you are feeling overwhelmed, you may be attempting to be a superhero. Accept that you are not. Asking for help is not a sign of weakness. Trying to be all things to all people is. When you ask someone for help, you are paying that person a compliment.

There are few surprises in this industry. The winners win because they deserve to. They know the path to success is traveled one step at a time, one day at a time. They concentrate on taking small steps each day to bring them closer to the future they dream about. They know what is important, when to ask for help, when to delegate, and when to say "No."

Decide what's important to you and put it at the top of your To-Do list each day. Don't waste time on minutiae that eats up time better spent achieving your goals, and don't spend your day darting from task to task.

Plan each day the night before so you can start working on productive activities first thing the next morning. Here's the best way I know to write an effective To-Do list:

1. Make a list of everything you want to do.

2. Do a reality check. Can you get everything done or do you need to move some items to another day?

3. If your list is overloaded, what needs to go?

4. Look for ways you can make your day smoother. Save time by writing the phone numbers next to the names you must call. Look for ways to combine two trips.

5. Rewrite the list with the most important tasks at the top.

Next morning, start early. If unexpected circumstances arise (how often have you said, "The day ran away on me" or, "I don't know where the time went"?), you will already have gone through a good portion of your list.

WORKSHEET **TWENTY**: MANAGE YOUR PRIORITIES

1. List the activities that fill your days now:

Business

_____

_____

_____

Personal

_____

_____

_____

Family

_____

_____

_____

Social

_____

_____

_____

Community

_____

_____

_____

Other

_____

_____

_____

2. Draw three columns and put each activity into one column depending how important it is to you.

YES = *Very Important*

_____

_____

_____

_____

_____

_____

NO = *Not Important*

_____

_____

_____

_____

_____

_____

MAYBE = *Somewhat Important*

_____

_____

_____

_____

_____

_____

3. Eliminate everything in your "No" column.

4. Eliminate everything in your "Maybe" column.

5. Start on your "Yes" column.

twenty-one

Don't Let Fear Trample Your Dreams

YOUR ATTITUDE WILL AFFECT YOUR ACTIONS, which will affect your results. It is almost impossible to be negative and move forward at the same time. Fear is disabling and destructive. It stops us from picking up the phone, seizing a golden opportunity to speak out about the business, servicing our customers regularly ("What if they say they don't like it?"), and building a team.

Every day I work in this industry I come across the same fears and anxieties. Perhaps you'll recognize one of the following personality traits in yourself:

Not Me's

"Not me's" believe that successful people are somehow different from the rest of us, and possess special qualities, rights, or advantages we lack. If you are one of the "not me's," you are in good company. Some of the industry's brightest stars started with loads of self-doubt. Most of us have periods of self-doubt from time to time. But perception is not reality. It's fantasy. You don't have to buy into negativity. Learn to put failures in perspective, by separating the issue from yourself personally. Think, "This is a failure," not "I am a failure."

Network marketing is one of the world's greatest equal opportunity businesses. Everyone has the same shot at success. Education, experience, ethnicity, gender, and previous jobs have nothing to do with what you can achieve.

Maybe some people are born under a lucky star. So what? The key is to work with what you have.

Label-Mabels

"I'm too young . . . too old . . . not confident enough . . . not a salesperson . . . too busy . . . too shy."

To my ear, these sound like excuses. Negative thinking leads to inaction. C'mon, this is not a dress rehearsal! We get one chance to live a full life and we can't afford to blow it. You are never too old or too young to start working on your dreams.

Maybe you tried other ventures that didn't work out so well. There is no value in looking back. The past is a dot in the distance. The future is the bright light ahead of you. Tear off those negative labels and start moving forward.

What-If'ers

Ever notice how we tend to get what we expect in life? Don't preempt failure by anticipating the worst. Think, "What if I fail?" and you are inviting failure. There is no more senseless way to spend time than worrying about what may happen. Remember Mark Twain's classic quip, "I've had some terrible times in my life, some of which actually happened." Does it ring a bell with you?

Setting yourself up to fail by focusing on the worst outcome is not only destructive; it's a complete waste of time and energy. You miss 100 percent of the hoops you don't shoot for. There are no penalties for not achieving your goals, so what do you have to lose? Go for it and you may just surprise yourself by achieving success beyond your wildest dreams.

Worrywarts

"Worrywarts" focus on what others think. Whoever said, "We would worry less about what others thought of us if we only knew how little they did," was onto something. So what if others doubt you or are waiting to see you fail? Most likely they are influenced by their own self-doubt or shortcomings. Ignore them, or better still, prove them wrong.

Not everyone is going to give you a positive response all of the time. Rejection is part of the process of sifting through prospects to find positive, enthusiastic people with big dreams who recognize the opportunity you are offering them. Only when we accept rejection as part of the job do we approach prospects without fear. Free yourself from caring what others think and you will surge forward.

Not Now'ers

What is the worst word in the dictionary? To my mind it's *when*.

Don't postpone your chance at success by procrastinating: "When the children go to school, when my partner changes jobs, when I lose weight, when I move house, when I finish school . . ."

There will never be a right time to pursue your dreams.

You will always be able to find a reason why *now* is the wrong time if you look for one.

If you have to work around challenges, that's life on Planet Reality. The alternative is blowing away your chances of living an amazing life.

The only fear worth holding on to is the fear of regret. Regret that you will one day look back at all the opportunities you didn't take because you let fear cripple you.

Achievers keep moving despite their fears and setbacks. They don't dwell on mistakes; they rebound from disappointment, and they refuse to let self-doubt destroy their dreams.

A healthy sense of humor helps. As does perspective. You have an opportunity to achieve success beyond your wildest dreams. You don't need to put up any capital. You don't need experience. You don't need to submit a resume or undergo a nerve-wracking interview. You don't need to compete against other people to take a shot at success. You have all the resources you want at your disposal. And you get to be CEO from Day One.

Tell me again, what is it you are worried about?

· ·

WORKSHEET **TWENTY-ONE**:
DON'T LET FEAR TRAMPLE YOUR DREAMS

· ·

1. Do you recognize yourself in any of these descriptions?

- ❑ Not Me's
- ❑ Label Mabels
- ❑ What If'ers?
- ❑ Worrywarts
- ❑ Not Now'ers

2. If you do, how are you going to deal with it?

_____

_____

_____

_____

_____

_____

3. Learn to laugh at yourself. Dig deep into your past to remember things you thought were problems then, and seem funny now.

4. Unshackle yourself from negative friends and surround yourself with positive people instead. You will find plenty in this industry, and you'll soon attract other optimists.

5. Don't give yourself time to wallow in self-doubt. The antidote to angst is action!

twenty-two

Fix What's Faulty

THERE ARE ONLY TWO REASONS why people fail in this business: not working hard enough or not doing it right. The most common fault is that they do not work hard enough. Success is 10 percent inspiration, 90 percent perspiration. If you are not working enough hours, it is unrealistic for you to expect to reach your target.

If you are working hard but still not seeing results, then you are not doing the right things. You may have the best intentions, but if it isn't working for you, it's time to find the fault and fix it.

Every move you make is working for you or against you. There is no neutral ground—your business will move forward or backward based on the actions you take.

Each of us has unique strengths that we can draw on, and each of us has our limitations. It makes sense to work from your strengths, and it makes just as much sense to eliminate the weaknesses that will hold you back.

Start by pinpointing where the problem is. If you are not meeting enough people, focus right there. If you have the leads but are struggling to find takers, do some serious work on your approach. If people join but don't perform, take a look at who you are recruiting, how you are training, and what support you are giving them. You will not move forward until you fix the weak links.

Never blame others for your lack of progress. Focus on yourself and what you can do. When you own the problem you own the solution. The key difference between people who make it to their destination and those who end up on the sidelines is the willingness to take responsibility.

No one gets a free ride. You may get one or two lucky breaks, but they won't exempt you from having to learn and apply the skills necessary to succeed.

Sometimes your technique may simply need fine-tuning, but be prepared to make major changes if necessary. If you have a flat voice, no matter how excited you are on the inside, people will not respond. Invest in voice coaching. If you don't know as much as you should about your products, use them more often and dig out the product manual. If there are aspects of your business you haven't yet grasped, make an effort to learn them. Knowledge bolsters confidence and credibility.

Be prepared to ask yourself tough questions: "Does my enthusiasm come across as pushy or desperate?" "Am I really a good listener or am I just waiting for a pause in the conversation so I can have my say?" You won't get far if you are broadcasting when you should be tuning in.

Can't pinpoint the problem? Swallow your pride and ask for honest feedback from people whose opinion you respect. Act on the advice you receive (and resist the urge to shoot the messenger!).

The stakes are too high for you to let your missteps determine your future, or to waste your chance at success by stopping when you reach the limit of your current knowledge, experience, or ability. Have the courage to rise beyond your previous performance peak, and you will reap the rewards.

WORKSHEET TWENTY-TWO: FIX WHAT'S FAULTY

Write down your answers to the following questions:

1. "What areas are working for me?"

_____

_____

_____

_____

2. "What areas are not working?"

_____

_____

_____

_____

3. "What practical steps can I take to address the areas that are not working?

_____

_____

_____

_____

_____

twenty-three

Lead by Example

THE HIGHEST EARNER IN NETWORK MARKETING I ever worked with had a simple philosophy: to set the pace and the example at every level on her company's compensation plan.

She always aimed to be the best consultant in her team, the best manager in her group, and so on, all the way up the line to the top tier of the company program. Did she need the recognition? Not after her home was overflowing with trophies. Did she need the money? Not after she had already become a millionaire many times over. Her motivation was simple: to show that it could be done!

Her powerful example to others took her to the top of the industry and empowered thousands in her downline. Success breeds success.

As your business grows so do your responsibilities. But if you neglect the basic activities that drive your business forward—scheduling, selling, and recruiting—how can you expect others to follow your example?

Never forget how you became successful in the first place and what a powerful example you can be to others.

This applies not just to driving your business forward but to the way you conduct your business. Don't underestimate the power of values to guide you through all the personal and business moves you will make in life.

Knowing where you stand, and what you stand for, makes life simpler. With a set of core values to guide you, you don't have to weigh up every new situation you encounter. Whether it's personal or business challenges you are facing, you simply apply your values and the solution will be self-evident.

Owning a business gives you a unique opportunity to create one that represents your highest personal and business values. The stronger your values, and the more consistently you apply them, the greater the credibility, respect, and loyalty that you will earn as you grow your business.

Imagine how you feel when someone you respect and admire approaches you. Excited? Flattered? Predisposed to respond positively to what she is saying? Of course.

Now think how this can work for you. Imagine that everyone you approach is flattered, excited, and eager to hear what you have to say. Leaders with charisma, credibility, and vision rarely fail to achieve their objectives in life.

Take the time to clarify the values that you will apply to all your business dealings, whether it is with your customers, your prospects, the people you introduce to the business, your corporate partner, or your suppliers. And why stop there? How you treat people who cannot do anything for you is a good indicator of the depth of your values. You cannot be selective if you hold true values. You have to apply them across the board.

Because your values will drive your actions, write them as statements:

- ★ "I will respect all my customers and recruits."
- ★ "I will never ask anyone to do what I am not prepared to do myself."
- ★ "I will always present the business honestly."
- ★ "I will never pressure people into making a decision."
- ★ "I will not set people up to fail by setting unrealistic expectations."
- ★ "I will honor all commitments."
- ★ "I will follow through on all promises."
- ★ "I will not be involved in any form of negativity."
- ★ "I will refuse to listen to gossip."
- ★ "I will return calls promptly."
- ★ "I will act on all correspondence quickly."
- ★ "I will pay my bills on time."

You gain a powerful business advantage by establishing standards from the start. Your business will be easier to manage, as your standards will effectively direct your actions.

If you have doubts about a decision you are about to make, take the "mirror" test. Ask the person in the mirror, "Am I proud of the way I am about to deal with this issue?"

If the issue is still cloudy, apply the family and friends test: "How would the people I care about view the action I am about to take?"

Credibility and trust must be earned. They are earned by openness, integrity, fairness, and honesty applied consistently (i.e., not just when others are watching, or when it suits). When you respect your company, your customers, and your associates, you will earn their respect in return.

By establishing and following clear guidelines, you will become a powerful role model for your business. The leadership you demonstrate will spread through your organization, strengthening your business every time others follow your lead. As goes the leader, so goes the team.

1. What qualities do you most admire in other people?

_____

_____

_____

2. What traits do you least admire in other people?

_____

_____

_____

3. How do you want others to describe you?
   a. Family and friends:

_____

_____

_____

   b. Your customers, upline, and downline:

_____

_____

_____

_____

_____

4. Which businesses do you least enjoy dealing with? Why?

_____

_____

_____

5. Which businesses do you most enjoy dealing with? Why?

_____

_____

_____

6. What lessons can you take from these businesses and apply to your business?

_____

_____

_____

7. List practical ways you will apply your values in the day-to-day running of your business. Be as specific as possible and make sure that you don't write anything down that you are not prepared to do every time whatever the circumstances or inconvenience.

I will not

_____

I will not

_____

I will not

_____

I will not

_____

I will not

_____

I will

_____

I will

_____

I will

_____

I will

_____

I will

_____

I will

_____

I will

_____

twenty-four

Keep Your Eye on the Ball

A HIGH PERCENTAGE OF PEOPLE who are attracted to direct selling are entrepreneurs, who love the concept of choosing when, how, and where they want to work, and having control over how much they earn. These "bright lights" bring energy, enthusiasm, and excitement to the business. They have amazing people skills and find it easy to fill their planners with appointments, from which they sell and recruit readily.

Their fire ignites their business quickly, but too often entrepreneurs fizzle out before they achieve true success. Why? It is because they lack the skills to maintain their business long term.

To reap the big rewards you have to be both a starter and a stayer. Attracting customers and representatives is one thing. Keeping them is another. Great businesses grow from a stable base, and that means looking after your customers so they keep coming back, and supporting the people you recruit so they stay.

However hard you have to work at it, maintaining relationships is always easier than repairing them. You will quickly burn out if you enter the relentless cycle of finding, losing, and having to find more people. The only way to ensure you are giving your customers the service you promise is to develop a simple system where you can see at a glance who needs following up.

People stay where they feel involved and appreciated, and where they achieve results. Most network marketing companies run on monthly or four-week cycles, enabling you to monitor your personal and team results throughout the period. Make sure you recognize achievements, guide those who are close to stepping up a level or achieving an incentive, and identify *hipo's*— that is, those who show the *highest potential* for growth. You won't succeed if you are an end-of-the-month manager, who only looks at the figures when it is too late to influence results.

The best approach to take in your business is "no surprises" management. Monitor who is flying and who is flagging on a weekly basis. When you know where your results are coming from, you know where to focus your attention.

The first ninety days of new representatives' lives are especially critical, as they transition from being excited and apprehensive to confident and capable. They need training, but even more, they need monitoring and support. By applauding their successes, helping them rebound from failures, and directing their next steps you will develop productive representatives. By keeping a close eye on performance, you will spot the red flags. A potential star who hasn't put in an order by midmonth, or who hasn't signed the new recruit whom he was so excited about, may have struck a snag. A little intervention before the situation gets out of control may save the day.

Keeping your eye on the ball isn't just about figures. It's

about taking a proactive approach to your business by reading all company communications to ensure you and your group don't miss out on key promotions and upcoming events, and so you can synchronize your efforts with your corporate partner's. It's also about spending a few minutes a day filing and record keeping, to save a lot of frustration at tax time. When you run your business from home you can deduct all your business-related expenses, including a percentage of your mortgage interest, rent, utilities, and maintenance costs. It pays to be organized with your receipts and expenses.

Take your business seriously. Monitoring and managing your business from the start will ensure you don't miss out on opportunities through neglect or oversight.

Great network marketers don't wait for things to happen or, worse, wonder what happened when their business spirals out of control. They make things happen through good business management.

WORKSHEET **TWENTY-FOUR**: KEEP YOUR EYE ON THE BALL

Review your systems:

❑   1. How well organized is your planner?

❑   2. Are you working the hours you promised?

❑   3. Have you set a specific time each week to check team results?

❑   4. Are you making follow-up calls in time to drive activity?

❑   5. Do you read all company communications?

❑   6. Do you run with every company promotion and event?

❑   7. Are your record-keeping systems working?

❑   8. Do you submit your returns to the IRS on time?

❑   9. Do you have your finger on the pulse of your business?

❑ 10. Are you encouraging your downline to follow your example?

STEP
twenty-five

Never Stop Learning

EVERY BEHAVIOR AND SKILL that increases your odds of building a successful network marketing business can be learned. Success is not a lottery. Although there will always be winners and losers, we can control which group we fall into by our willingness to learn and apply the skills.

This is a dynamic industry, and every change can be turned into a business advantage. New products will lead you to new customers and new customers will lead you to new recruits. New trends will open up new opportunities.

If you fall into the habit of doing things the same way, over and over, you will miss out on all the advances that drive this business forward. Opening yourself up to new ideas and information will keep your business fresh and exciting and keep you on a fast track to personal growth.

Although training is no substitute for learning on the job, there is no better investment you can make than in yourself.

Attend every training session offered to you, and register for company seminars and conferences. Rather than try to digest all the information you receive, look for key points that you can put to work. One new idea implemented will produce better results than a host of new ideas in a closed notebook. And don't count training hours as work hours. Whatever your schedule, never neglect your customers, prospects, and recruits.

In the early stages of my business, I found that tuning in to other people through books, seminars, and tapes gave me the encouragement I needed to stay focused. Their energy and enthusiasm were as motivating and uplifting as their ideas. Hearing top achievers sharing the challenges they faced helped me put my own experiences into perspective.

There is a wealth of material available at bookstores and libraries, and *Monday Mentor*, my e-zine for network marketers, offers ongoing training, encouragement, and support via your e-mail in-box (see the end of Step 26 for details). The more you learn, the more resources you will have to draw on. One year's experience repeated five times over is not five years' experience. If you do the same thing five years in a row, you may have wasted four of those years. Building on your skills and knowledge through trial and error will equip you to deal with the inevitable up-and-down cycles, changes in the economy, and the changing needs of your customers and representatives.

Seize every opportunity to associate with talented, like-minded people. Their expertise and outlook will rub off on you, just as yours will on them. Don't waste time with negative or unmotivated people who will drag you down.

Excellence is a moving target. No matter how successful or busy you become, don't neglect the key person in your business: yourself. Set aside a small percentage of your earnings, and a small amount of your time each day, for education and personal development.

The day you stop learning, you stop growing. The day you stop growing, your business will start to stagnate.

WORKSHEET **TWENTY-FIVE**: NEVER STOP LEARNING

1. Ask your colleagues and upline managers to recommend books, audiotapes, or CDs that have helped them. List the titles for future reference.

_____

_____

_____

_____

_____

2. Start your own library of self-help books. When you are not reading them, pass them around your group.

3. Listen to training or motivational CDs when you are driving.

4. Note upcoming training events in your planner and commit to every one.

5. Promise yourself that you will not borrow from work time to pursue education and personal growth.

twenty-six

Have Fun

THERE ARE BASICALLY TWO TYPES OF ACTIVITIES: those you enjoy doing and those you don't. From the grim faces of the office warriors commuting to and from work each day, it's safe to say that for most people work falls into the second category.

Not so in this business. Network marketers enjoy what they're doing—mostly because they have control over their time, their income, and their life. They know that when the going gets tough, they are still better off than the average worker, who is pummeled by long hours, demanding employers, office politics, and salary increases that trail inflation.

If you are an executive or employer, you know that the tensions don't subside just because you're on the management team. Many will argue it gets worse, not better, because the pressure to compete is greater.

Either way, you will discover that working for yourself is

a dream in itself. Not least because of the two-second commute to your office; working in the clothes you choose to wear; making appointments that avoid rush hours; enjoying quality time with your partner; playing your favorite CD in the background; being home for the kids after school; and, above all, having the freedom to decide how and when you will work.

When you work for yourself, you have no excuse not to be happy. And researchers are quick to point out that happy people are more likely to be successful.

Happiness is a mind-set. You can choose to be the type of person who lights up a room when you enter it, or you can choose to be someone who lights up the room when you leave.

Decide that building your business will be a fun experience.

Start with your expectations. If you expect a Fantasy World where nothing goes wrong, then you are setting yourself up for disappointment. If you commit to succeeding on Planet Reality, where the best plans come unstuck, appointments get cancelled, you drive ten miles in the rain to a no-show, your star recruit leaves, your brilliant prospect turns out to be a turkey, your partner phones to say he's working late when you are counting on him to babysit . . . you'll make it to your destination.

We get what we give. Be warm and respectful to difficult and delightful customers alike. Love your demanding recruits as much as your gems. See difficult situations as character building! Don't rush. It takes just one minute to make someone feel special with your undivided attention.

Liven up your presentations. Most people would rather be entertained than lectured to. Hold fun meetings. We learn best when we're having fun. Actively seek out happy people, and cross the street to avoid the miserable and mean-spirited ones. Celebrate every milestone, no matter how small.

Stress is a major turnoff. Make sure you come across as relaxed, no matter how busy you are. Not only will you feel better; you'll look better too. There's nothing like stress for digging lines into the face, and nothing like relaxation for ironing them out.

Look for ways to increase the "fun factor" in your life and in your business, and you will become a beacon for other enthusiastic, fun-loving people who want to enjoy what they do.

WORKSHEET TWENTY-SIX: HAVE FUN

1. Look for reasons to laugh—you'll succeed faster, live longer, look better, and enjoy life a whole lot more.

2. Cultivate perspective. The situation is as dire as you choose to make it.

3. Start celebrating your future by congratulating yourself for completing this study course. If you send me an e-mail (mary@marychristensen.com), I'll send you my congratulations, along with a complimentary copy or two of *Monday Mentor*, my e-zine for direct sellers and network marketers.

A FEW FINAL THOUGHTS

I WROTE THIS BOOK to show that you have as much chance of succeeding, and as much right to succeed, as anyone. The power to change your life is in your hands.

✶ ✶ ✶ ✶ ✶ ✶

The most remarkable aspect of network marketing is that it does transform lives: the lives of people like you and me—everyday people with big dreams, and the drive, determination, and discipline to see them through.

✶ ✶ ✶ ✶ ✶ ✶

Because this is a people business I can almost guarantee you some tumultuous times. There will be days when you will feel as if you are on a roller coaster as your business peaks, dips, and curves. But that's the nature of network marketing.

✶ ✶ ✶ ✶ ✶ ✶

I hope I have inspired you to set your sights high, and to find the courage, know-how, and strength to make your dreams come true.

> Whatever you can do, or dream you can, begin it.
> Boldness has genius, power, and magic in it.
>
> —Johann Wolfgang von Goethe

INDEX

abbreviations, avoiding, 80
achievements, recognizing, 124
action(s)
    translating knowledge into, 5
    values as drivers of, 118–119
Amway, 28
anticipation of problems, 110–111
anxieties, 109
    see also fear(s)
appearance, personal, 81
appointments
    ease in making, 56–57
    limiting length of, 76
    scheduling, 55–56
asking for help, 105
associates, 2
attention, keeping, 81
attention spans, 80
attitude(s)
    fear-based, 109–112
    shift in, 2
    for success in business, 97–98
auto-ship programs, 61

balance
    in mentoring, 90
    in recruiting, 84–85
belief(s), 16–23
    acquisition of, 17
    self-doubt vs., 16–17
    for success, 98
    taking responsibility for, 17–18
    worksheet for, 20–23
Binary compensation plans, 29
blame, 98, 115
blue hat, 67
brain, sides of, 18
Breakaway compensation plans, 27–28
breakaways, 26, 85, 89
building relationships, 53
    see also relationships
bulk messages, 94
business owners, 2
business ownership, 2
    benefits of, 3–4
    costs of, 3
    values expressed in, 118

business partner, corporation as, 37
business-related expenses, deducting, 125
business seminars, 77
buying privileges, in Hybrid Unilevel/ Unigen plans, 38

calls, making, 48, 56, 58
calmness, radiating, 67
cancellations, overbooking to cover, 56
capital investment, 3
careers, alternatives to, 2
celebrating milestones, 131
changes, need for, 4
charisma, 118
Churchill, Winston, on giving in, 99
closing sales, 61–63
colorful communication, 80
commercials, length of, 75–76
commissions
    in Binary plans, 29
    in Hybrid Unilevel/Unigen plans, 38
    in pyramid schemes, 34
    in Stairstep/Breakaway plans, 27
commitment to goals, 11
communication
    in developing/maintaining relation-
        ships, 71–72
    developing skills in, 79–82
    with downline, 72–73
    with eyes, 81
    for radiating positive energy, 66–68
    self-talk as, 17–18
    in selling, 61–63
    simplicity in, 75–76
    visual, 80–81
    voice quality in, 81, 115
    worksheet for, 82
compatibility of goals, 11–12
compensation plans, 24–36
    basic principle of, 25
    Binary, 29
    breakaways in, 26

"breaks" in, 32
    comparing, 31–33
    Forced Matrix, 28–29
    Hybrid Unilevel or Unigen, 28
    pyramid schemes vs., 33–34
    ranks in, 25–26
    Stairstep or Breakaway, 27–28
    structures of, 26–27
    understanding of, 25, 29–30
    worksheet for, 34–36
compliments, 18
conferences, 128
confidence, 20, 67
consideration of others, 18
consistent work hours, 48
consultants, 2
continuous learning, 127–129
core skills, 52–54
    advanced, 53
    basic, 52–53
    and success of business, 52
    worksheet for, 54
corporate partners, 2
    synchronizing efforts with, 125
    training program of, 5
    unique attributes of, 38
corporate resources, 37–42
    and compliance with corporate sys-
        tem, 39
    mistakes in, 38
    worksheet for, 40–42
corrections, making, 102
costs of network marketing, 3
courage, 20
credibility, 118, 119
criticism, filtering, 18
customers
    building loyal base of, 60
    flexibility in dealing with, 102–103
    following up with, 63
    keeping vs. finding, 71
    maintaining relationships with, 123, 124

overexplaining to, 76
relationships with, 61, 71
responding to issues of, 61
staying in touch with, 61

David (statue), 19
depth, 29
desire, recruits with, 85
direct selling, see network marketing
Direct Selling Association, 2, 33
discipline, 105
discounts, 31, 32
distributors, 2
downline, 25
    developing relationships with, 71–73
    flexibility in dealing with, 102–103
    see also recruits
dreams, 6–9
    postponing, 111–112
    realizing, 1
    value of, 7
    visualizing, 7–8
    worksheet for, 9
drive, recruits with, 85
DSA Code of ethics, 32

e-mails, 94
emotional thinking, 18
employment alternatives, 2
energy
    focusing, 10
    from passion, 7
    positive, 66–69
    worksheet for radiating, 68–69
enjoying work, 130–132
enthusiasm, 115
excellence, 128
excuses, 4, 98–99, 110
expectations, 131
expenses, deducting, 125
eyes, communication through, 81

fact, separating fantasy from, 18
failure
    most common reason for, 47–48

of new companies, 102
perspective on, 110
reasons for, 114
setting yourself up for, 111
simplicity as way to avoid, 75
fairness, 119
family life, 1
fantasy, separating fact from, 18
faults, fixing, 114–116
fear(s), 109–112
    of "label-Mabels," 110
    of "not me's," 109–110
    of "not now'ers," 111–112
    of regret, 112
    of "what-if'ers," 110–111
    worksheet for, 111–112
    of "worrywarts," 111
feedback
    asking for, 115
    positive, 18
filtering, of criticism, 18
financial independence, 1, 2, 86
first levels, 25, 26, 73
fixing problems, 114–116
    and reasons for failure, 114
    worksheet for, 114–116
flexibility, 101–103
    importance of, 101
    worksheet for, 103
follow-up to sales
    after online communications, 94
    discipline for, 71
    to ensure customer satisfaction, 63
    system for, 124
Forced Matrix compensation plans,
    28–29
Ford, Henry, on belief, 16
forgiveness, 18
front-end loading, 32
fun, 130–132

"games" (in pyramid schemes), 33
get-rich-quick schemes, 34

goals, 10–15
    amending, 103
    defining and setting, 11–12
    momentum for achieving, 97, 98
    priorities in, 104
    purpose of, 10
    realistic, 10, 12
    worksheet for, 12–15
Goethe, Johann Wolfgang von, on
        dreaming, 134
growth potential, 124

happiness, 131
    questions for defining, 7
    radiating, 67
hats, as basis in impression-making, 67
help, asking for, 105
hipo (highest potential for growth), 124
home, working from, 2, 3, 130–131
honesty, 119
hours dedicated to working, see work
        hours
humor, sense of, 112
Hybrid Unilevel compensation plans, 28
hype, 80

imagination, 6–7
impact, 76
impatience, 10–11
impressions, positive vs. negative, 66–67
improvements, making, 47
income, 3
    from discounts, 32
    residual, 47
    see also compensation plans
independent representatives, 2
insecurity, 18
integrity, 119
international businesses, 31
Internet, 93–95

jargon, avoiding, 80
judgment of others, 18

kindness, 19
knowledge
    actions based on, 5
    building on, 128
    continuous learning for, 127–129
    of products, 115

"label-Mabels," 110
labels, negative, 17
language, simplicity of, 80
leadership, 117–122
    recruits with potential for, 85, 89
    values in, 118–119
    worksheet for, 120–122
learning, continuous, 127–129
levels (of recruits), 25
limited matrix plans, 28
limits, 6, 7

maintaining relationships, 124
management
    as core skill, 53
    "no surprises," 124
    of priorities, 104–106
    stress in, 130
    technology as aid for, 94
    worksheet for, 125–126
    of your business, 123–126
marketing plans, see compensation plans
markets, unpredictability of, 101
markups, 31
Mary Kay, 28
mastering skills, 99
McDonald's, 39
measurable goals, 11
meetings, fun in, 131
Melaleuca, 29
members, 2
mentoring, 89–92
    as core skill, 53
    worksheet for, 91–92
Michelangelo, 19

milestones, celebrating, 131
"mirror" test, 119
MLM, *see* network marketing
momentum, 97–100
Monday Mentor e-zine, 128
monitoring business, 123–125
multilevel marketing, *see* network marketing
myths, 80

negative impression, creating, 66
negative self-talk, 17
negative thinking, 20, 110
negativity, 110
network
    adding to, 56–57
    nurturing relationships in, 71
    qualities of people in, 128
network marketing, 2–3
    basic principles of, 4–5, 47
    benefits of, 1, 3–4
    costs of, 3
    income from, 3
    international, 31
    most common reason for failing in, 47–48
    reasons for working in, 2
    volatility of, 102
newsletters, e-mailing, 94
"No," saying, 105
"no surprises" management, 124
"not me's," 109–110
"not now'ers," 111–112
numbers (in recruiting), 84
Nu Skin, 28

online sales, 93–94
openness, 119
opportunity nights, 77
overbooking, 56
overexplaining, 57, 76
owning problems, 115

partnerships with corporations, *see* corporate partners
passion, 7
payments
    on discount vs. markup, 31
    on wholesale vs. retail prices, 31
    see also compensation plans
personal appearance, 81
personal development, 129
    see also continuous learning
personal group, 25
personal growth, 20
perspective, importance of, 112
planners, 55, 56
    see also scheduling
plans, *see* compensation plans
points systems, 31
positive energy, radiating, 66–69
positive impression, creating, 66–67
positive self-talk, 17–18
Power Hour, 48
presentations, livening up, 131
priorities, 104–108
    of goals, 11
    setting, 104
    To-Do lists for, 105–106
    worksheet for, 106–108
proactive approach to business, 125
problems
    applying values to, 118
    fixing, 114–116
    flexibility in handling, 101–103
    owning, 115
    working through, 43–44
procrastination, 48, 111–112
productive times of day, 48
product refunds, 32–33
products
    knowledge of, 115
    personal use of, 60
prospects, flexibility in dealing with, 102–103
pyramid schemes, 33–34

quality of life, marketing, 67

radiating positive energy, 66–69
ranks (compensation plans), 25–26
rational thinking, 18
realistic goals, 10, 12
record keeping, 72
recruiting, 83–88
  broadening base for, 86–87
  as core skill, 53
  importance of, 83
  mistakes in, 83–84
  rules of, 84–85
  width and depth in, 83
  worksheet for, 87–88
recruits
  being honest with, 80
  in Binary plans, 29
  breakaways, 26
  in business partnership, 39–40
  first ninety days for, 124
  in Forced Matrix plans, 28–29
  in Hybrid Unilevel/Unigen plans, 38
  individual goals and characteristics of,
    40
  with leadership potential, 85
  loving, 131
  maintaining relationships with, 124
  mentoring, 89–91
  in pyramid schemes, 33
  ranks of, 25
  in Stairstep/Breakaway plans, 27
  "star," 84–85
  see also downline
red hat, 67
referrals, asking for, 57
refund policy, 32–33
regret, fear of, 112
rejection, 20, 58, 111
relationships, 70–74
  building, as core skill, 53
  with customers, 61
  with downline, 71–73

  with first levels, 73
  keeping records of, 72
  maintaining, 124
  mentoring, 89–91
  in network, 71
  worksheet for, 73–74
relaxation, 67, 132
repeat business, 63
residual income, 47
resources of corporate partner, see corporate resources
responsibility
  during bad times, 43–44
  modeling, 117–118
  for personal beliefs, 17–18
  for problems, 115
  worksheet for, 44–45
  for your success, 43–45
results, trying vs., 4–5
retail price, payments based on, 31
role modeling, 119
  see also leadership

sales
  closing, 61–63
  as foundation of network marketing,
    60
  income and, 25
  ranks based on, 25–26
  sources of, 32
  via Internet, 93–94
  see also selling
saying "No," 105
scheduling, 55–59
  and adding to personal network,
    56–57
  of appointments, 55–57
  as core skills, 52
  overbooking in, 56
  of work hours, 55
  worksheet for, 58–59
self-centeredness, 79
self-discipline, 105

self-doubt, 7, 16–17, 110
self-esteem, 18, 20
self-reliance, 2
self-restraint, 105
self-talk, 17–18
selling, 60–65
    as core skill, 53
    steps in, 61–63
    worksheet for, 63–65
    to yourself, 60
seminars, 77, 128
Shaw, George Bernard, on dreaming, 8
shipping, 61
shortcuts, 4
simplicity, 75–78
    core skills for, 52
    worksheet for, 77–78
skills
    building on, 128
    communication, 79–82
    core, 52–54
    mastering, 99
spillover, 29
Stairstep compensation plans, 27–28
standards, establishing, 119
"star" recruits, 84–85
strategies, amending, 103
strengths
    focus on, 19
    working from, 114
stress, 132
success
    attitude for, 97–98
    beliefs for, 98
    core skills for, 52–54
    and hours worked, 47
    leadership for, 117–119
    more success bred from, 117
    path to, 105
    postponing chance for, 111–112
    qualities needed for, 123
    radiating, 67
    responsibility for, 43–45

tapes, training, 128
technology, 93–96
    as competitive edge, 93
    using Internet, 93–95
    worksheet for, 96
teleconferencing, 94
teleseminars, 94
To-Do lists, 105–106
top down close, 62–63
training
    corporate programs for, 5
    for downline, 72
    investing in, 127–128
trust, earning, 119
trying, results vs., 4–5
Twain, Mark, on anticipating problems, 110–111

uncertainty, 7
Unigen compensation plans, 28
upline, 38
USANA, 29

values, 118–119
visual communication, 80–81
visualization of dreams, 7–8
voice coaching, 115
voice quality, 81, 115

warmth, 67
weaknesses
    eliminating, 114–116
    working on, 20
wealth, 1, 4
Web conferencing, 94
websites, maintaining, 93–95
"what-if'ers," 110–111
wholesale price, payments based on, 31
women, attitudes shifts in, 2
words, minimal use of, 75, 76
work hours, 46–51
    appropriate use of, 47
    consistency in, 48

work hours (*continued*)
   maximizing effectiveness of, 49–50
   scheduling, 55
   and success of business, 47–48
   training time separate from, 128
   worksheet for, 50–51
worksheet
   for beliefs, 20–23
   for communication, 82
   for compensation plans, 34–36
   for continuous learning, 127–129
   for core skills, 54
   for corporate resources, 40–42
   for dreams, 9
   for fears, 111–112
   for fixing problems, 114–116
   for flexibility, 103
   for fun, 132
   for goals, 12–15
   for leadership, 120–122
   for management, 125–126
   for mentoring, 91–92
   for momentum, 99–100
   for priorities, 106–108
   for radiating positive energy, 68–69
   for recruiting, 87–88
   for relationships, 73–74
   for responsibility, 44–45
   for scheduling, 58–59
   for selling, 63–65
   for simplicity, 77–78
   for technology, 96
   for work hours, 50–51
"worrywarts," 111

yellow hat, 67

ABOUT THE AUTHOR

MARY CHRISTENSEN has more than twenty years of network marketing leadership. *Be a Network Marketing Superstar* is based on her own success in the direct selling industry—from successful party planner; to building her own direct selling business and recruiting more than 1,000 people in her first year; to leadership roles in two multinational network marketing companies.

A former president of the Direct Selling Association, Mary originated one of the world's first university courses in network marketing, authored *Make Your First Million in Network Marketing*, and founded *Monday Mentor*, a coaching e-zine for direct sellers worldwide.

Today she is a sought-after keynote speaker who appears at the industry's most prestigious events, as well as at a host of corporate conventions every year.